The FORTS of OHIO

A GUIDE TO MILITARY STOCKADES

❖

Gary S. Williams

Buckeye Book Press
Caldwell, Ohio
2003

Photos by Owen Williams

Please direct all correspondence and book orders to:
Gary S. Williams
42100 Township Road 491
Caldwell, OH 43724
Phone: (740) 732-8169 or (740) 732-7291
email: buckeye_books@earthlink.net

Library of Congress Control Number 2003102034
ISBN: 0-9703395-1-8

Published for Buckeye Book Press by
Gateway Press, Inc.
1001 N. Calvert Street
Baltimore, MD 21202-3897

Printed in the United States of America

TABLE OF CONTENTS

INTRODUCTION

By 1814 the Indian wars that had made wooden stockades a frontier necessity for over sixty years were over. In that year, William Henry Harrison called for treaty negotiations to be held with all tribes who had allied themselves with England during the War of 1812. The site he selected for talks was Fort Greeneville, where, 19 years earlier, he had served as an aide to General Anthony Wayne when Wayne had obtained the treaty that made Ohio safe to settle. Harrison was so intent on repeating Wayne's success that he insisted that his headquarters be on the very spot that Wayne's had been.

Harrison was not the only one to feel that this ground was special. His rival, the great chief Tecumseh, whose death in combat with Harrison's army the previous autumn had a lot to do with peace being possible, had felt similarly. In 1805, Tecumseh and his brother, The Prophet, had built their village on the site of Fort Greeneville specifically to defy the treaty dictated to his people here.

Anthony Wayne himself had also made ceremonial use of special locations. On Christmas Day of 1793, he had a fort built on the spot where, two years previously, an Indian coalition had inflicted upon Arthur St. Clair's troops, the worst defeat ever suffered by the U.S. Army. Wayne named this post Fort Recovery.

Harrison, Tecumseh, and Wayne were the three greatest leaders involved with the early forts of Ohio, and among the characteristics they shared was a strong sense of site. Be it reverence for sacred ground or pursuit of a psychological advantage, these leaders appreciated that historical sites held great significance.

This is just as true today, where we need to be reminded of some of these places that hosted so much of Ohio's early history. From 1750 to 1815, log forts played such a prominent role in this story that "forting up" became the determining factor of survival for the early white intruders. Yet no directory exists of the early forts of Ohio. This book aims to fill that void.

As heritage tourism becomes increasingly popular, there is a need for a traveler's directory to these sites of significance. The accounts that follow will discuss all of the federal fortifications built in the state during this era. Emphasis will be on the fascinating people who served here, what happened on the spot, and what is on the site today. The illustrations included will therefore show what the ground looks like today, rather than offer artist's versions of the original forts.

The approximately 65-year-period where log forts were built in Ohio was an era of constant upheaval. In 1750, there were only a handful of white men interacting with the native Indians whose trade was sought by European rivals England and France. Yet by the end of the War of 1812, the Indians were relinquishing their claims to the United States. Ohio was the first state to be settled by American citizens. The forts built here by the fledgling U.S. Army had tremendous significance, since, at the time, it was seriously doubted that the new nation could protect its westward expansion. The triumph of this process and the people who made it possible is the story told here.

Some decisions had to be made to define the focus of this book. In general, the forts described here were log stockades constructed under federal auspices and garrisoned with regular troops who were part of a larger military campaign. Not included are palisaded trading posts, armed camps, blockhouses and community stockades built for protection. While a directory of all these outposts would be an excellent topic for a book-- one has already been done on the stations of the Symmes purchase-- it is not the subject of this one. This is also not a scholarly work, although it does take advantage of the research done by those who have delved into the primary sources and official records.

The forts are arranged in the approximate order that they were built, rather than in alphabetical or geographical order. This way, reading the book in order gives an overview of Ohio's early tumultuous military history. Of the 33 forts included here, only five were ever attacked, and the only one to be captured and destroyed was taken from within. Some posts included here were only briefly-held supply depots, while others were the scene of great drama.

There is a similar diversity in the condition of the sites today. Some locations are unknown or unmarked, although most at least have a historical marker nearby. The Anthony Wayne Parkway and the Daughters of the American Revolution have been particularly diligent about placing markers at significant locations. Other sites are city or state parks with appropriate monuments, and a select few have even been rebuilt or have museums. All of these locations need to be presented in one volume so that Ohio's collective sense of site can be better preserved.

ACKNOWLEDGMENTS

In the course of doing research, I have found that librarians everywhere are universally helpful, and to them I would like to issue a blanket thank you. Among other specific people who offered advice, information or encouragement, I would like to mention the following: Bob Hirche, Ann Hughes, David Osborne, Roger Pickenpaugh, Phil Ross, David Simmons, Brian Williams, Drew Williams and Larry Zachrich. A special thanks goes to Terry Mullins for the great job she did on the index.

Closer to home, this effort has been a family project. My daughter Meryl was chief typist and my son Owen was art director in charge of illustrations and layout. My wife Mary continues to serve as consultant and as life partner, and excels in both roles. And guidance and enthusiastic support was received from my father, M. Leslie Williams. I'm pleased to have written the kind of book he likes to read, and I respectfully dedicate this one to him.

The Forts of Ohio

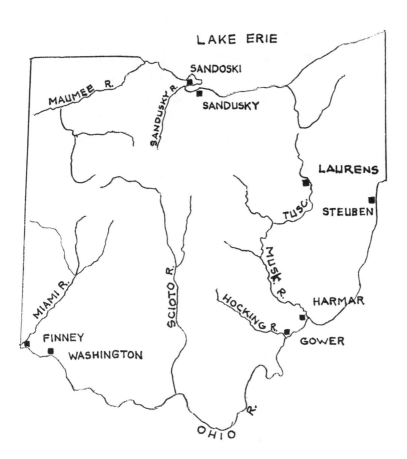

LAKE ERIE

EARLY FORTS
OF OHIO

1

The Forts of Ohio

EARLY FORTS OF OHIO

Prior to 1788 the only white people living in Ohio were either living among the Indians or inside of forts. There were no permanent settlers within the state's eventual borders, but the soldiers stationed in the forts were involved in a complex struggle for control of the region that would determine future settlement.

France and England were rivals for the lucrative Indian fur trade, and the British also envisioned future colonization. Both sides had palisaded trading posts, but the first fort to host soldiers was probably the only Ohio fort built by non-English speaking people.

After defeating the French, the first Ohio fort built by the British was destroyed in Pontiac's Conspiracy. The British regained control of the region only to be challenged by Americans seeking independence. The Indians correctly saw that the Americans were a greater threat to take their land and most sided with the British.

After the Revolution, the United States tried to use Ohio lands as currency to reward veterans and subsidize their new government. With both Spain and England claiming bordering land and Indians occupying Ohio, it was crucial to the future of the new country that this venture succeed. But the U.S. army was pitifully small and poorly equipped and could barely staff a few isolated outposts along the Ohio River.

The Forts of Ohio

FORT SANDOSKI

The first fort built in what is now Ohio may have been the only one not built by English-speaking people. Fort Sandoski was constructed by the French around 1751 on the north shore of Sandusky Bay in Ottawa County. It was possibly built on the site of an English trading post dating to 1745, and the controversy surrounding the first fort in Ohio mirrors the conflict between the French and the British for the region.

The Ohio country was central to the struggle between the two powers. As the English colonists grew more numerous along the Atlantic coast, they looked to expand across the Appalachian Mountains. The French were far less numerous, but they controlled the mouths of the St. Lawrence and Mississippi Rivers, the largest known on the continent. By going up the St. Lawrence to the Great Lakes, and then down the Ohio and Mississippi it was possible to travel by water from Quebec to New Orleans with only brief portages around Niagara Falls and between the Ohio and Great Lakes watersheds. The French hoped to hem the British in via this water route and thereby maintain supremacy in the lucrative fur trade with the Indians of the North American interior.

All streams in Ohio flow either into Lake Erie or the Ohio River watershed, and there are several places in the state where the headwaters of the respective watersheds are only a short portage apart. The French were the first to discover this as LaSalle had sailed on Lake Erie and down the Ohio in the 1670's. They sought to build a series of posts to protect these water routes.

English fur traders threatened the French plan. While the French traders generally had a better rapport with the Indians, the British had superior and cheaper trade goods. The French felt sufficiently threatened by 1749 that they sent a force of 300 soldiers and Indians under Celeron de Bienville into Ohio. This first military expedition into Ohio traveled down the Ohio and up the Miami Rivers, and with great fanfare placed lead plates at major river junctions proclaiming ownership for France. They also stopped at all Indian villages and drove out any British traders.

At the village of Pickawillany, at the site of present day Piqua in Miami County, they found the British firmly entrenched. Traders there had already built a private stockade and the local Miami chief was aligned with them so strongly that he was known as Old Britain. The village ignored French warnings, and in 1752 French led Indians from Michigan attacked the village, scattered the traders, and "made a broth of" Old Britain, which is to say they boiled and ate him.

There were pro-British Indians elsewhere, including the Sandusky region not far from the French fort at Detroit. The term Sandusky can be confusing, as, for example, Upper Sandusky is south of Sandusky, and neither town is in Sandusky County. "Sandusky" generally refers to the area drained by the Sandusky River and Sandusky Bay. In this area, a Wyandot chief named Nicolas allowed British traders to build a blockhouse in his village around 1745. As was the case at Pickawillany, this structure had a corporate rather than a military function, and no soldiers were ever there.

The French forced Nicolas to leave the area and in 1751 built Fort Sandoski, possibly near his former village. Unlike the British, French trade efforts generally included a military presence, and a garrison of around 20 troops was stationed here during the fort's brief lifetime. The site of the fort was at the bottom of the neck of the Marblehead Peninsula in Erie County. It is just two miles from the mouth of the Portage River at Port Clinton to the northern rim of Sandusky Bay. The portage that the fort guarded here saved 50 miles of sailing or paddling around the mouth of Sandusky Bay and provided a quicker route to the land along the Sandusky River. This is believed to be the approximate location, though no trace of the fort remains today.

Fort Sandoski was used only briefly, as a French officer named De Lery mentions it being abandoned in 1754. By that time, the French had also established a trading post on the southern rim of Sandusky Bay. Some maps referred to this post as Fort Junandat, and others did not call it a fort. De Lery, who was a military engineer, makes reference only to traders at this post, so it is likely that this was a civilian facility used for the fur trade only. The post at Junandat was used until 1759, and it is believed the first white child born in Ohio was born here.

The French were busy building posts that definitely were military forts at this time. They built a series of forts in western Pennsylvania in 1753 that guarded key points along a Lake Erie-Ohio River portage line. The Virginia colony sent a youthful militia colonel named George Washington with a letter asking them to vacate lands claimed by Virginia. Instead, the French moved on to build Fort Duquesne at the forks of the Ohio. The next year, when Washington attacked a French advance party, he was pursued by a large French force and forced to surrender at Fort Necessity. The following year the British sent regular army troops, but the Redcoats under General Edward Braddock were annihilated almost within sight of Fort Duquesne.

It wasn't until 1758 that the more numerous British and Americans were able to succeed under General William Forbes, who renamed the post Fort Pitt. The next year the British captured Quebec, and in the Treaty of Paris of 1763 the French were forced to relinquish all claims in North America. Henceforth, English was the only language spoken by soldiers in Ohio.

FORT SANDUSKY

Of the nearly forty forts built in Ohio, only five were ever attacked, and only one of these successfully. That was Fort Sandusky, the first fort by the British in Ohio. And like the only other Ohio fort built by British troops, its very construction was a blatant treaty violation.

When the capture of Montreal occurred in 1760 at the end of the French and Indian War, the British took

The Forts of Ohio

possession of the French forts scattered across the Great Lakes. British commander General Jeffrey Amherst immediately sent off British troops to occupy these forts. This expedition was led by Major Robert Rogers and was the first British sponsored military operation into Ohio. Rogers was the leader of the famous Roger's Rangers, an elite corps of American fighting men so used to combat in all conditions that they had even fought on snowshoes and on skates. Rogers and his men followed the southern shore of Lake Erie and had a testy encounter with a then unknown chief named Pontiac at the mouth of the Cuyahoga. When Rogers got to Sandusky Bay, he wrote the French commander at Detroit demanding he turn it over to the victorious British. This was accomplished before the winter snows fell, and the British assumed control over ten isolated forts from Erie, Pennsylvania to Green Bay, Wisconsin.

The British were supposed to keep only the existing forts, but it was decided to build a new one on Sandusky Bay, where the Indian trail between Fort Pitt and Detroit met Lake Erie. In August of 1761, Fort Pitt commander Colonel Henry Bouquet ordered Lieutenant Elias Meyer and 38 soldiers of the Royal American Regiment to "Sandusky Lake" to "build a small Block house with a Palisade around it, to serve as a Halting Place for our Party going and coming from Detroit."

Lieutenant Meyer selected a location on the southern shore of Sandusky Bay near its mouth. The most likely spot seems to be in the present-day village of Venice, just outside Sandusky in Ottawa County. A historical marker notes the spot at the junction of State Route 6 and Venice Road. The isolated crew worked through the fall, encountering problems with provisions and such matters as getting a stone mason who could build what had to be one

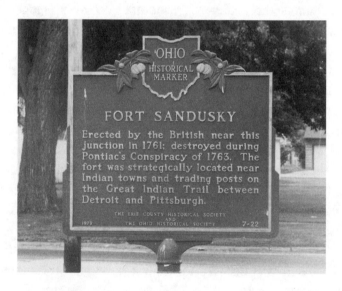

of the first chimneys in Ohio. Meyer wrote to Bouquet, "rest assured, Sir, that I shall neglect nothing to finish it as soon as possible, so as to be delivered from this purgatory." They finally completed construction at the end of November. In February of 1762, a skeleton crew of fifteen soldiers was left under the command of 24-year-old Ensign Christopher Pauli (sometimes spelled Paully).

An Ensign was the lowest rank of a commissioned officer, below lieutenant and just above sergeant. The

The Forts of Ohio

British had too many spread-out forts to garrison and so few troops available that only one other fort besides Pitt and Detroit had more than 30 men on duty or was headed by an officer with a higher rank than lieutenant. The fact that Fort Sandusky was new construction contributed to the bad feeling the midwest tribes had about the British. While the French traders formerly living among them treated them as equals, the haughty English turned the forts into armed camps, having learned that trading posts required a defensive force. And without the two countries to play off each other, the natives found themselves at the mercy of a British monopoly to obtain such vital supplies as blankets and gunpowder. Disgruntled Indians disliked the new order and thought the time was right for action.

The Great Lakes tribes could not believe the French had given up so easily, and hoped to bring them back into the picture. The Ottawa chief Pontiac assembled an eighteen tribe coalition that planned to attack all the western forts in the spring of 1763. The surprise attack that Pontiac himself was supposed to lead against Detroit was revealed to the British, but Pontiac's Conspiracy met with unprecedented success everywhere else. Of the ten forts west of Fort Pitt, Detroit was the only one not destroyed.

Fort Sandusky was the first to fall. While at other forts the Indians used such stratagems as betraying mistresses and a staged game of lacrosse to gain entrance through the gates, such subterfuge was not necessary here. On the morning of May 16, 1763, a group of Indians asked to be let in for discussions, and Pauli, unaware of the siege

The Forts of Ohio

already under way at nearby Detroit, let them in. After a ceremonial smoking of a peace pipe, a chief gave a signal and Pauli was suddenly seized. The rest of the garrison was quickly and quietly killed, along with about a dozen traders. As he was bound and led off for Detroit, Ensign Pauli could look back and see his fort burning.

Pauli had every reason to expect the same fate, since his captors taunted him about it. But after being forced to run the gauntlet and being prepared for death, he was instead adopted into the tribe that had taken him. Indian custom allowed captives to be spared if they were named to replace departed family members. Although he was rescued Pocahantas style, the widowed squaw who saved Pauli was apparently neither young nor beautiful. He was adopted into the tribe and joined the attackers who were besieging his fellow soldiers. Here he remained until he escaped to the fort on July 3.

A British relief party en route to Detroit found the ruins of Fort Sandusky and the mutilated bodies of the garrison, and they attacked a nearby village in retaliation. But the siege of Detroit lasted until November, a tribute to Pontiac's tenacity and organizational skills. However, Pontiac eventually had to accept that the French were not coming back, and if the Indians were to get all the trade goods they had come to depend on, they would need to make peace with the British.

The next year, the British sent out two large forces to maintain the peace. One group, under Colonel John Bradstreet, sailed along Lake Erie, and negotiated settlements with individual tribes that further confused the issue. This group stopped and camped at the site of Fort Sandusky. They began work on a replacement fort but abandoned the project well before completion.

The other force, under Colonel Henry Bouquet, marched into Ohio with a well trained army of 1,500 men. This large and disciplined force demanded the return of all captives taken during Pontiac's Conspiracy and over 200 captives were repatriated at the present site of Coshocton. After this confrontation, the unsettled frontier remained peaceful for a decade, enforced by a British policy that forbade forts and settlement in the Ohio country.

FORT GOWER

Fort Gower is a study in contrasts. The Athens County fort was built by order of one English Lord and named for another, yet all the troops there were backwoods Virginians. And although little more than a briefly used cattle pen, from that crude stockade came an eloquent Ohio-based Declaration of Independence that preceded the definitive version by a year and a half.

Fort Gower was built during Lord Dunmore's War, a Virginia-led campaign that culminated in a battle that some have called the first battle of the American Revolution. This was in 1774, when both Virginia and Pennsylvania were claiming the region around Fort Pitt. Settlers were forbidden to move across the Ohio River by the King's Proclamation of 1763. In addition, the Quebec Act of 1774 made the

The Forts of Ohio

Ohio country a part of the province of Canada. This particularly angered the frontiersmen who had fought the French for this country only to see Parliament return it to Canadian control.

A series of incidents in the spring of 1774 led the Virginians into a war that they hoped would strengthen their claims to western lands. The most serious of these occurred on April 30th, when whites lured a group of Indians across the Ohio near present-day Steubenville and murdered them. This group included the family of the Mingo chief Logan, who had previously been a friend of the whites. But now he took to the warpath seeking revenge, and soon the frontier was in turmoil.

Taking advantage of this situation was Lord Dunmore, the last royal governor of the colony of Virginia. He raised two separate militia armies, one of which under Colonel Andrew Lewis was sent up the Kanawha River towards the Ohio. The other force was led by Dunmore himself, and was at the site of Fort Pitt in August. They started down the Ohio where they were to meet up with Lewis. Dunmore sent a party ahead under an officer named William Crawford to build a fort at the mouth of the Hocking River.

Crawford was a good friend of George Washington. The two had met as teenagers on a surveying expedition in 1749, and would remain friends until Crawford's horrible death in 1782, when he was burned at the stake by Indians seeking revenge for the Gnadenhutten Massacre. In 1770, the two had traveled down the Ohio looking for possible bounty lands for French and Indian War veterans. They had camped at the mouth of the Hocking River, and Washington had expressed interest of the fertile bottom lands of the area. Now Crawford wrote Washington on September 20th, 1774, joking that "I am this day to set out... to erect a post on your bottom."

Crawford selected a spot on the east bank of the mouth of the Hocking, in the current village of Hockingport, although archaeological digs have failed to come up with an exact location. His 500 men began building a rude stockade with but a single blockhouse. The fort was to be used for the storing of the army's livestock and canoes, and the stockade may never have been completed. Dunmore arrived with about 1,000 more men, and named the fort for Lord Gower, a political crony in Parliament.

As they were preparing to set out for the Ohio interior, unbeknownst to them, Lewis' 1,500-man force was attacked at Point Pleasant in West Virginia at the mouth of the Kanawha. After a fierce battle on October 10th, the Indians retreated and realized they could not prevent the two armies from uniting. Dunmore left 100 men at Fort Gower and went up the Hocking to present-day Logan and cut across towards the Scioto River. At Camp Charlotte in Pickaway County, he was able to dictate peace terms to all major chiefs except one. The exception was Logan, who refused to attend, and under an elm tree, gave an impassioned oration saying he was through avenging the deaths of his family members. Logan's Lament has been used as an example of Indian eloquence.

The Forts of Ohio

Dunmore's victorious Virginians returned to Fort Gower in early November. They knew that tension with the British was high and "having lived three months in the woods without any intelligence from Boston, or from the delegates at Philadelphia," the expedition's officers met to discuss a response to their concerns. They voted to issue a resolution to King George stating their beliefs.

In the preamble to the Fort Gower Resolves, the troops expressed pride in their recent efforts, and boasted that, "our men can march and shoot with any in the known world." Indeed, Point Pleasant was the first time an army of Americans had defeated the Indians without help from British troops, which is why some call it the first battle of the Revolution.

Concerning their loyalties to England, the Resolves stated they would "bear the most faithful allegiance to his Majesty King George the Third, whilst his Majesty delights to reign over a brave and free people," but warned, "But as the love of Liberty and attachment to the real interests and just rights of America outweigh every other consideration, we resolve that we will exert every power within us for the defense of American liberty."

The Fort Gower Resolves were approved on November 5th, 1774--over five months before Lexington and Concord and more than a year and a half before the Declaration of Independence. Among the officers who approved them were three who would become generals in the American Revolution. Adam Stephen apparently took a leading role in the process and would become a Major

The Forts of Ohio

General in Washington's Army. Two other officers-Daniel Morgan and George Rogers Clark-would go onto glory in the War for Independence. Morgan played a heroic role in American victories at Saratoga and Cowpens, while Clark saved the Northwest Territory from British control with his capture of Vincennes.

The Fort Gower Resolves were taken back and printed in the Virginia Gazette in December. They were later reprinted in colonial newspapers in North Carolina, Pennsylvania, Connecticut, and Massachusetts. The Resolves had no teeth, but were similar to other statements issued around the same time. But this version emanated from the backwoods of Ohio. Today there is a DAR marker

at the corner of Grand and Orange Streets (near the junction routes 124 and 144) in Hockingport to mark the spot of the fort where Ohio's Declaration of Independence was issued.

FORT LAURENS

In the American Revolution, Ohio was no-man's land. Situated between American western headquarters at Fort Pitt and the British at Detroit, Ohio was filled with Indians whose allegiance was sought by both sides. Most Ohio tribes favored the British, who had more gifts to offer them and were less of a threat to steal their land. Also, the outnumbered Indians could not afford to back a losing horse and felt that the British were more likely to win. Tribes allied with the British raided American settlements in Kentucky, Virginia, and Pennsylvania. They were even paid a bounty for American scalps by Detroit commander Lieutenant Colonel Henry "The Hairbuyer" Hamilton, a policy which enraged the Americans.

The Americans still sought alliances with the Indians, which were essential if they hoped to traverse Indian lands to capture Detroit. In September of 1778, they invited all tribes to a treaty conference at Fort Pitt, but the nearby Delaware was the only tribe to show any interest. The Delaware nation agreed to allow American troops to pass through their territory and to build a fort there.

In late October of that year, a 1,200-man American army under General Lachlan McIntosh left Fort Pitt. Their goal was to take Detroit by following the Great Trail that led across Ohio to Sandusky Bay. They stopped two days later to wait for supplies and constructed a post called Fort McIntosh in western Pennsylvania. Then, on November 4, they set out for the Ohio country following the route used by Henry Bouquet in 1764.

But this was no disciplined army like Bouquet's had been. The Americans lumbered and blundered across the terrain and were further slowed by a herd of cattle they were driving to use as a food source. It took them two weeks to get to where the Great Trail crossed the Tuscarawas River at present-day Bolivar--an average of about only five miles a day.

The Americans realized an attack on Detroit was out of the question and it was too late in the year even to attack the hostile tribes of the Sandusky region. After a council of war, McIntosh decided to build a fort and use it as a launching pad to march on Detroit in the spring. This would also honor their pledge to build a fort to protect the Delaware and the Moravian mission towns, even though the principal Delaware and Moravian towns were near Coshocton, 40 miles to the south.

Accompanying McIntosh's army was the Chevalier de Cambray-Digny, a French officer who had offered his service to America. Trained as an engineer, he designed the new fort and it was therefore more substantial than previous forts that had been, although it still would not have been able to withstand an artillery attack. The fort covered about an acre of ground, or about 240 feet square. There were two gates, four bastions, and a ditch surrounding on all but the side facing the river. A total of eleven buildings were eventually built in and around the fort. The post was christened Fort Laurens, in honor of Henry Laurens, president of Continental Congress and a friend to McIntosh.

The partially completed fort was left to the care of Colonel John Gibson and 180 men of the 13th Virginia regiment. The rest of McIntosh's army left on December 9th, when there was already six inches of snow on the ground. Gibson proved to an excellent choice to command the isolated post, as he had the respect of both his troops and the Indians. The Delaware had even requested his presence, saying at the Fort Pitt treaty, "it is our particular request that John Gibson may be appointed to have charge of matters between you and us. We esteem him as one of ourselves; he has always acted as an honest part by us and we are convinced he will make our common good his chief study and not think only how he may get rich."

Gibson earned this trust in a long career that featured a prominent role in nearly every frontier conflict over a 50 year period. He served in the French and Indian War on the Forbes campaign and then remained in the Fort Pitt areas as a fur trader. Captured during Pontiac's Conspiracy he was saved from being burned at the stake and married the sister of Chief Logan. She was among those murdered at the beginning of Dunmore's War. Gibson served with Dunmore as a translator and was the man to whom Logan addressed his famous lament. Gibson was in command at Fort Pitt by the time of Cornwallis' surrender and later succeeded William Henry Harrison as Governor of Indiana Territory during the War of 1812.

McIntosh had threatened the Indians with American might, but the natives could clearly see through him when they saw how poorly provisioned the Continental Army was. The garrison was poorly clothed, had no shoes, and didn't have enough nails to finish the fort. They soon became dependent on the Indians they had been sent to protect. A group requesting supplies at Coshocton was fired upon and had to be accompanied by a contingent of pacifist Moravian converts to guarantee their safety.

As their condition worsened in the harsh winter, Gibson wrote to Fort Pitt describing the situation. Unfortunately, on January 22, 1779, a party returning to Fort Pitt was attacked by Indians under the leadership of the notorious renegade Simon Girty. Two men were killed and the soldier carrying Gibson's letter was captured. The messenger was taken to the Sandusky region to be burned alive and the dispatches convinced the British that the fort was weak enough to be attacked.

Moravian missionaries warned the fort of its impending attack, but a group of nearly 200 Mingos, Wyandot, and a handful of British soldiers still managed to approach the fort undetected. On the morning of February 23, the attackers announced their presence by capturing a seventeen man wood-cutting detail outside the fort's gates. They then killed and scalped their captives in full view of the horrified garrison. Then they further demoralized the garrison by repeatedly parading through a forest opening to create the illusion that they had 847 warriors present.

By a strange coincidence, George Rogers Clark was employing the same trick on Henry Hamilton at Vincennes, Indiana, on the same day. But while Hamilton was convinced to surrender without a shot on February 25, Gibson refused to fall for the trick. Fort Laurens held out for nearly a month under horrible conditions.

When food rations had been depleted, the troops were reduced to boiling and eating their own moccasins. Two men died from eating poisonous roots. When a hunter was fortunate enough to bring a deer into the fort, the famished soldiers pounced on it and devoured it raw.

The Americans at Fort Pitt tried to send a relief expedition under Major Richard Taylor, whose son Zachary would go on to become President. But the overland Bouquet route was considered too risky, and Taylor instead tried to go down the Ohio and up the Muskingum. But Indian attacks and high water forced him back well short of his goal.

Legend has it that Gibson relieved the siege by offering the Indians a barrel of flour if they would leave. He reasoned that the attackers would grow discouraged if they felt the garrison had its flour to spare, so he scraped up his last barrel in a successful effort. There is no confirmation of this story and it's possible that the Americans simply outlasted the Indians, who had little patience for winter time siege warfare.

The Forts of Ohio

A larger overland relief expedition in the meantime had been sent from Fort Pitt, and they rescued the starving troops on March 23. However, the overjoyed defenders turned this into tragicomic relief by firing their guns in celebration and stampeding the pack horses that were to be used in the assault on Detroit. After a council of war, it was decided to abandon further operations. Gibson and his men were replaced by 100 troops from the 8th Pennsylvania under Major Frederick Vernon.

McIntosh was soon replaced as western commander, and his successor had little use for the fort he called "the hobby horse on the Muskingum". The isolated post suffered from supply problems and scattered Indian attacks even during the warm months, and the fort was ordered evacuated on August 2, 1779.

The fort decayed over the years and part of the site was covered by the Ohio and Erie Canal. In 1915, the state of Ohio purchased 81 acres around what was believed to be the original site to use as a park. In 1970 the Ohio Historical Society decided to build a museum and interpretive center on the site. An archeological dig looking for artifacts in 1972 discovered the exact location of the fort close enough to the museum that some artifacts were lost. The outline of the fort is marked today and the park also hosts many reenactment weekends, and on the grounds is the tomb of Ohio's unknown Revolutionary War soldier.

A group called the Friends of Fort Laurens has hopes of getting Ohio's only Revolutionary War fort rebuilt. The site is located just south of State Route 212 at the Bolivar exit of Interstate 77 in Tuscarawas County.

FORT HARMAR

At the dawn of Independence, the mighty U.S. Army consisted of fewer than 1,000 soldiers, the largest part of which was stationed at a star shaped fort at the mouth of the Muskingum River. Even stranger is the notion that the fort was built to protect Indians from white settlers. But these are the facts about Fort Harmar, the first fort built by soldiers from the army of the new United States of America.

The Forts of Ohio

When England agreed to recognize U.S. Independence in 1783, there was no longer a need for the Continental Army. The Americans had a distrust of peacetime standing armies and considered them oppressive, especially since they had previously been forced to house and feed occupying British soldiers in their homes. Many in the new country felt the nation's military needs could be met by calling out the state militia in times of crisis. A handful of regular professional soldiers would be needed to guard federal arsenals only. By 1784, the entire U.S. Army consisted of 55 soldiers at West Point and 25 more at Fort Pitt. The highest-ranking officer was a captain.

But there were some, most notably George Washington, who felt that some sort of peacetime army would be necessary, especially in the west, where the British and Spanish threatened American annexation of land occupied by natives. The British were expected to surrender the Great Lakes forts they had taken from the French, and troops would be needed to man these posts if the nation was supposed to expand its western borders. Continental Congress authorized the formation of a regiment in 1784 with the stipulation that its federalized troops come from the volunteer ranks of existing state militia. As Pennsylvania provided the most men to that force, their militia leader, Josiah Harmar, was given command of the army with the rank of Colonel.

Harmar's men refurbished Fort McIntosh, a few miles downstream from Fort Pitt. An Indian treaty was signed here on January 21, 1785, where the U.S. asserted the right to settle lands across the Ohio River. Actually, hundreds of people were already living on the Ohio side, but these squatters did not hold legal title to the land they occupied. The first mission of the new army was to clear out illegal settlers so legal settlement could proceed.

A force under Ensign John Armstrong went through the area in March to evict the squatters, but many of them reoccupied their cabins after the troops left. A more permanent military presence was needed on the spread-out frontier, and on October 5, 1785, Harmar ordered Major John Doughty and 140 men to proceed down river to build a fort to enforce to U.S. policy. The site Doughty selected was on the west bank where the Muskingum meets the Ohio in present-day Marietta.

The Forts of Ohio

Doughty's fort was more elaborate than most frontier forts. The post had five bastions instead of the usual four and it was the first Ohio fort to have artillery, with cannons mounted to cover the broad sweep of the Ohio River. The logs on the outer walls were stacked horizontally, and the bastions were built to a height of fourteen feet. The inside of the compound covered only about three fourths of an acre, but included barracks, a two-story building for officers, an arsenal, store house, a tower to overlook the river, and a well. The main gate overlooked the Muskingum with a secondary "sally port", facing the hill side. Although the fort was not completed until the following spring, on November 30, 1785, Doughty was able to report to Harmar that "we have nearly completed the barracks and stockade, and the men are all in." He named the fort for his commanding officer.

Fort Harmar became the headquarters for the U.S. Army in 1787-1788. As more settlers poured downstream, it became wise to move the army as well and Harmar stationed himself and the bulk of his troops at his eponymous fort. At this time, the entire Department of Defense consisted of Secretary of War Henry Knox, three clerks, and a messenger. In the absence of military structure in the capital at New York, it could be said that the five sided Fort Harmar was the country's first Pentagon.

But what the country's prime military post was best known for was its gardens. Doughty had laid out extensive gardens behind the fort in his original plans, and the fertile soil yielded an abundance of beans, peas, squashes, and melons. Fruit trees were also planted and a variety of peach tree known as the "Doughty peach" originated at the fort. Jonathan Heart, an officer in the garrison wrote to a friend back East "I do not exaggerate when I declare the Soil in its present Situation is more Luxuriant than than the best manured gardens in Wethersfield (Connecticut)."

The good farming conditions were what attracted settlers to the new frontier. But it was no coincidence that the first permanent settlement in the Northwest Territory was located within sight of the largest fort on the frontier. On April 7, 1788, the garrison welcomed a group of 48 New England pioneers who landed on the eastern side of the Muskingum and founded the town of Marietta. On July 9, newly appointed Territorial Governor Arthur St. Clair arrived to initiate civil government.

St. Clair's first order of business was to assure safe settlement with a treaty agreement with the various tribes. He originally called for treaty talks to reaffirm the concessions made at Fort McIntosh to be held at the Falls of the Muskingum at present-day Duncan Falls. But when his supplies there were attacked by Indians, St. Clair decided to hold the talks at Fort Harmar. Late in 1788, chiefs from the various tribes were escorted to the fort by the soldiers, although the most belligerent tribes, such as the Miami and Shawnee, did not send representatives. Those who did attend were a disunited lot of lesser chiefs who were coerced and bribed into ratifying the American rights to settle in most of what is now Ohio. The Treaty of Fort

The Forts of Ohio

Harmar was signed on January 9, 1789, and was supposed to guarantee safe settlement of the new territory, but as most Indians did not accept it, the treaty hastened a general warfare.

This treaty also led to a celebrity residing at Fort Harmar when noted frontiersman Lewis Wetzel was imprisoned there. Wetzel, whose hatred of all Indians was as well known as his scouting skills, was charged with shooting one of the Indian delegates to the treaty conference. Wetzel was celebrated as an Indian killer, but there were two unusual things about this shooting: one was that in this case, his victim actually survived and recovered, and the other was that, this time, Wetzel found himself arrested rather than congratulated.

While Wetzel's skills were unsurpassed at tracking down Indians and liberating captives, he did not confine his killing to wartime. He also killed Indians in public encounters in peacetime, and this time his work threatened to undermine peace negotiations. Harmar sent a contingent of troops with orders to arrest Wetzel, but the scout was shielded by settlers who were outraged that the federal government wanted to prosecute a hero merely for shooting an Indian. But when Wetzel later returned to the Marietta area he was captured and taken to Fort Harmar in irons. Wetzel had previously escaped from Indian captivity and he was able to escape federal custody as well. After being permitted to exercise in the fort, he suddenly climbed the walls while still in handcuffs and escaped to the sympathetic populace, who hid him.

The Forts of Ohio

Wetzel's killing skills were soon back in vogue in the general Indian warfare that engulfed the Ohio region from 1790 to 1794. In the fall of 1790, most of the garrison was transferred to Fort Washington at Cincinnati, where Harmar was planning to launch an offensive against the Indians. A small garrison of around 50 men was left under the command of Captain Haskell to protect the settlers during the ensuing Indian wars. After the Greeneville Treaty of 1795 there was no longer any need for Fort Harmar, and the post was abandoned.

Erosion has caused much of the site of Fort Harmar to fall into the Ohio River. Today, the Harmar Elementary School is at the confluence of the Ohio and Muskingum Rivers. A marker at the junction of Fort Street and Fort Square marks the approximate location of the fort that was once the headquarters of the U.S. Army.

FORT FINNEY

It is possible that Fort Finney was the first fort built by the newly organized United States government. The men who built it left two days before the expedition to build Fort Harmar did and although they had to travel much farther, there is evidence that it was constructed and occupied before the more elaborate Fort Harmar. But since Fort Finney was used only for about nine months it is easily overlooked.

The most significant event at the fort at the mouth of the Great Miami River was the signing of the Treaty of

The Forts of Ohio

Fort Finney on January 31, 1786. This coercive treaty and its aftermath had more effect on the settling of Ohio than did the ephemeral fort.

It was October 3, 1785, that Colonel Harmar sent a company of 70 men under Captain Walter Finney downstream on the Ohio. The mission was to build a post approximately where Ohio, Indiana, and Kentucky come together. There were no legal settlers in this area yet, but Kentuckians were eagerly eyeing the fertile lands north of the Ohio. To facilitate settlement, the new government needed to establish clear title to the lands from the Indian occupants.

Accompanying the soldiers were Indian Commissioner Richard Butler and a 27-year-old Congressman named James Monroe. Butler was to negotiate a treaty with the Indians, while the ambitious Monroe was on a fact finding tour of the west. The future President returned to Virginia through Kentucky before the fort site was reached. By then the group had been joined by George Rogers Clark.

Finney's men traveled downstream on 12 keelboats that were also laden with supplies. They were accompanied by two flatboats that carried the horses, cattle, and other stock that the expedition would use. Low water on the Ohio that fall made progress slow and they traveled only about twelve miles per day. On October 22, they arrived and selected a site about 150 yards from the Ohio, although one source says the fort may have been a mile upstream on the Miami. It is known that the fort was built on the eastern bank of the Miami even though Clark had expressed a preference for the western bank.

Work progressed swiftly and within three weeks the troops had completed a stockade about 100 yards square, with four 24 by 18 foot bastions that served as barracks. A powder magazine and storehouse were added later, as was a council house located outside the stockade. The new post was christened Fort Finney in honor of the Captain.

With the new fort in place, the Americans summoned area tribes to it for treaty negotiations. But when representatives of the Shawnee tribe arrived, they found that there was little room for negotiation. The American position was that the Indians had forfeited any rights to the land they occupied by aligning with the defeated British. The Treaty of Paris, in which the British recognized the U.S. Government, made no mention whatsoever of the Indians, so the subject was wide open to interpretation. By treating the Indians as an already conquered people, the Americans hoped to be able to open Ohio for white settlement without even offering compensation.

On January 14, 1786, over 300 Shawnee convened at the council house outside the fort. The festivities began amidst military pomp that included a twelve gun salute from an honor guard and martial music. While the Americans later realized it was probably better to offer a token payment for land concessions, at the treaty this was not the case. American commissioners Butler and Clark threatened to walk out at the first sign of protest. The war-weary and isolated Shawnee tribe agreed to nearly every American demand, including the rights to most of what is now Ohio.

The dull fort life on the isolated frontier was not broken by many events. But according to Ebenezer Denny, an officer in the garrison who kept a diary, St. Patrick's Day was a notable exception. He noted that many of the troops were Irish and on this day they were permitted to drink as much whiskey as they could purchase. The result was that one man drank so much he died from alcohol poisoning.

In August of 1787, Fort Finney was abandoned as the garrison moved downstream and built a new Fort Finney at the Falls of the Ohio opposite Louisville. The short-lived fort didn't last as long as repercussions from the treaty that was negotiated there.

In the summer of 1786, settlers in Kentucky were subjected to a series of Indian raids, mainly from the Miami tribe located in Indiana. To retaliate they sent raiding parties of their own. One group under Clark went toward the Miami villages, but another under Benjamin Logan struck at the Shawnee. This group destroyed many Shawnee villages, including one that was flying the American flag. Moluntha, a friendly chief who had signed the Treaty of Fort Finney was murdered in cold blood after he had given himself up to the Kentuckians.

This raid enraged the Shawnee and hardened their attitude against the Americans. They became a significant part of a formidable coalition of tribes that soon brought settlement of Ohio to a standstill. Richard Butler, who had negotiated the Treaty of Fort Finney, became one of the victims of the new attitude. As General St. Clair's second-in-command, he was one of the many Americans killed at St. Clair's disastrous defeat in 1791.

During the ensuing period of Indian warfare, frantic settlers on the north side of the Ohio demanded federal troops to protect them. Handfuls of soldiers were dispatched to various stations and blockhouses, and the abandoned Fort Finney site was temporarily re-occupied. The troops here must have been an undisciplined lot, as the local name for the site during this time was Camp Rowdy.

After the Greenville Treaty was signed the site of Fort Finney fell into decay. No trace remains of the fort today.

FORT STEUBEN

Though it was occupied only for seven months, Fort Steuben played a role in the nation's history. The post at the present site of Steubenville helped launch a national land survey system that was used throughout the winning of the West.

At the end of the American Revolution, the British renounced all claims to what became the Northwest Territory. The new United States was counting on sale of these lands to keep the country afloat financially. However, the Natives currently occupying those lands were not consulted in any of this.

The Forts of Ohio

Before any land sales on settlement could occur, the area had to be surveyed. To facilitate this, Continental Congress passed the Land Ordinance of 1785. This document specified that the new lands were to be divided into townships that were six miles square. Each township would be broken into 36 sections that were one mile square each, or 640 acres. Although it wasn't until 1787 that any law was passed regarding governance of the new territories, the Land Ordinance did specify that one section of each territory be used to benefit public education.

The man responsible for conducting the first land survey was William Hutchins, the Geographer of the United States. In 1784, Hutchins had surveyed the western boundary of Pennsylvania from Lake Erie to the southern state boundary line that had been drawn by British surveyors Mason and Dixon in 1768. The point where the Ohio River crossed this line was to be the beginning of the new survey. In the fall of 1785, Hutchins began plotting a line due west from this point for 42 miles, with all land south of the line to make up the first seven ranges of townships. However, rumors of Indian unrest soon halted work for the year.

The following year, the work was continued with additional survey crews from other states, many of which included speculators and investors who later played a role in the Northwest Territory. The survey crews were understandably worried about Indian attacks and requested federal troops to protect their efforts. Colonel Harmar ordered three companies under the command of Major John

Hamtramck to stand guard over the various survey crews. As the crews became increasingly spread out, and as Indian unrest increased, it was decided to build a centralized fort for protection.

On October 11th, 1786, Hamtramck selected a spot on a terrace overlooking the Ohio at a place called Mingo Bottom. The surveyors would soon disperse for the winter, but the fort would house the 150 protecting soldiers until spring. Hamtramck was of French and Belgian extraction and he came to America by way of Canada. His sister was the wife of Alexander MacKenzie, the Canadian explorer who first crossed North America twelve years before Lewis and Clark. Hamtramck joined the American forces during the Revolution and although he didn't speak the language well, he did understand how to motivate his men.

With only one blockhouse completed and winter fast approaching, he offered incentive to his troops. He assigned each company to complete a blockhouse and offered six gallons of whiskey to the company who finished first, with four gallons for the second place company. The men who finished their blockhouse last would have to dig the ditch for the pickets. The race began on Friday, October 27, and all three blockhouses were completed by noon on Sunday.

The soldiers spent their first night in their new quarters on November 4. They got in just in time as a harsh early winter hit and there was two-and-a-half feet of snow on the ground a month later. The winter came on so fast that a boatload of troops crossing the Ohio had to walk back when the ice froze and locked their boat in. The walls and finishing touches on the fort could not be completed until a January thaw. At this time, Hamtamck named the post for Baron Von Steuben, the recently retired Inspector General of the Revolutionary Army. From his New York farm, Steuben wrote that he was "touched at this new mark of attachment of my old army friends."

Fort Steuben was a compact fort of simple design. The four blockhouses were 25 feet square and doubled as barracks for the enlisted men. They were set out at 45 degree angles from the pickets. Also on the grounds were officers' quarters, a commissary, quartermaster's store and magazine, and a blacksmith shop. A gate overlooking the river also had a guard house.

Colonel Harmar only visited his newest fort once, and Hamtramck often was absent himself, as he made trips to both Forts Pitt and Harmar. The enlisted men were not going anywhere, partly because they were so poorly supplied that they did not have adequate shoes or clothes to travel outside of the fort.

The surveyors were anxious to begin working, and some crews started as early as February. As warm weather arrived, the survey crews demanded increased protection. Harmar complained to Knox that the surveyors were "extravagant in their demands... the whole regiment would scarcely provide for them." By now the crews were in the southern portions of the Seven Ranges and could be better protected by soldiers from Fort Harmar. On May 23, Fort

Steuben was ordered to be evacuated and the garrison headed downstream to other forts a week later.

The land survey system developed in the Seven Ranges was used throughout all western expansion. Fort Steuben itself, however, served only as a decaying landmark and a source of wood and nails for new settlers. The city of Steubenville grew up around it, and the site was forgotten for nearly 200 years. But today the fort has been rebuilt by the Old Fort Steuben Project, a private non-profit organization.

The group purchased the site off State Route 7 in 1986 and raised the funds to rebuild the buildings of the fort and part of the palisade. The group hosts Fort Steuben Days in June and has plans to complete the fort and add a visitor's center.

The Forts of Ohio

FORT WASHINGTON

Most of the forts built in Ohio were only used for a few years and several of them were functional only for a few months. The exception to this was Fort Washington, where the post was used for almost the entire territorial era. From 1789 to 1804, Fort Washington played a significant role in Ohio's history, launching three major Indian campaigns and being responsible for the city of Cincinnati growing up around it.

As the U.S. Government offered land for sale, it became apparent that the average man lacked the cash to make the minimum purchase of 640 acres, and corporate intermediaries were needed. One such company under the leadership of Judge John Symmes of New Jersey purchased a large portion of land covering the 27 miles between the mouths of the Little Miami and Miami Rivers. In the fall of 1788, the first group to settle this region came west, and almost immediately requested federal protection for their exposed position.

After the Treaty of Fort Harmar, the army saw that they were more likely to be needed further downstream, and plans were made to move their headquarters away from Fort Harmar. In August of 1789, Harmar sent a company of 70 men under Major John Doughty to select a suitable site for a fort. Existing settlements at the mouth of the Little and Great Miami Rivers were logical locales, but after careful scouting, Doughty selected a spot opposite where the Licking River flowed up from Kentucky and entered the

Ohio. It was a shallow spot often used as a ford by both white and Indian raiding parties. The exact location was on the second terrace above the river, and out of the flood plan, near the current intersection of Third and Broadway.

An additional company was sent from Fort Harmar in September and construction was supervised by Captain William Ferguson. The fort was built with a stone foundation and reinforced planking to hold off artillery attacks. The wood used was from discarded "Kentucky boats" that had served their function of bringing new settlers to the area. The fort was a 200 foot square with two-story frame buildings inside and two-story blockhouses at each corner. Later, triangular enclosures with a blockhouse were added to the north and west sides of the fort. The main gate faced the Ohio and in the center of the grounds was a well and flagpole. The southeast blockhouse served as military headquarters.

General Harmar arrived with 300 additional troops at the end of December, and was pleased with the progress. He wrote to Secretary of War Knox that, "this will be one of the most solid, substantial wooden fortresses, when finished, of any in the Western Territory. On account of its superior excellence, I have thought proper to honor it with the name of Fort Washington." On January 2, 1790, Governor St. Clair arrived at the site and did some naming of his own. The village around the fort had been called Losantiville, a convoluted name meaning the village opposite the mouth of the Licking. St. Clair promptly rechristened the town Cincinnati, after the Order of

The Forts of Ohio

Cincinnatus, an organization of Revolutionary War officers, in which he was an active member.

Fort Washington became important militarily as it became apparent that the various treaties were not going to hold. As Indian raids increased, a military expedition was planned to punish warring tribes in the fall of 1790. Harmar's small army was little more than an understaffed police force, so it was necessary to call out militia from the Kentucky settlements to head up the Licking to Fort Washington. On September 30, Harmar led a force of 350 regulars and 1,100 militia out of the fort and into Indian country.

This cumbersome, slow moving force was watched all the way by Indian scouts. In addition, St. Clair had written the British at Detroit to tell them of the expedition and to reassure them of the limits of his intentions. The British had shared the information with their Indian allies. Consequently, the Americans found only abandoned villages as they headed north. They burned lots of crops but encountered no Indians until they got to the site of present-day Fort Wayne, Indiana.

Here a group of Americans was lured into an Indian ambush. The untrained and undisciplined military promptly threw down their loaded muskets and ran, leaving the now outnumbered regular troops to be cut to pieces. Three days later another portion of the American army fared no better in battle. The Americans returned to Fort Washington on November 4 and claimed victory, even though they'd had 183 soldiers killed in battle. But it became apparent from the immediate increase in Indian raids that the allied tribes were encouraged by their success, and were therefore the real victors.

The next year the Americans decided to try mounted raids before raising a large army. A group of monted Kentuckians led by Colonel James Wilkinson left Fort Washington on August 1, 1791 and covered an average of 21 miles per day for the next three weeks. Captives from this raid, mainly women and children, were held as hostages at the fort.

That fall Fort Washington was the gathering place for an expedition to be led by St. Clair, who was made a Major General for the occasion. But troops and supplies were slow to arrive and St. Clair did not leave Fort Washington until September.

St. Clair was anxious to achieve some sort of results before winter set in. But the result was the annihilation of his poorly trained army. On November 4, 1791 the Americans were surprised along the Wabash River, with losses that amounted to over 900 of 1,400 troops. It was the worst defeat ever suffered by a U.S. Army.

Panic now spread on the frontier and Indian confidence soared to new heights. St. Clair resigned his commission as general, although he retained his job as governor. His place at Fort Washington was taken over by James Wilkinson, who accepted a commission as a Brigadier General.

Wilkinson was a popular Kentucky-based leader who had been a general in the Revolution. But what no one knew was that he was a spy in the pay of the King of Spain. From 1787 until his death in 1825, Wilkinson accepted thousands of dollars in gold and silver as Agent Number Thirteen to supply the Spanish with information and to use his influence on Spain's behalf. Wilkinson was on the Spanish payroll while serving as the commander of the U.S. Army, and while he plotted with Aaron Burr, and after he turned Burr in and offered the chief testimony against him. Burr was acquitted of treason but the chief witness against him was definitely guilty of it.

As terror spread across the frontier, new settlement came to a standstill and pioneers already here holed up in privately built stockades. In the Ohio Company purchase areas, these stockades tended to have eloquent names such as Campus Martius (Latin for "field of war") in Marietta and Farmer's Castle in Belpre. The most isolated post on the Muskingum at Big Bottom, which did not follow this trend, was wiped out by Indian attack on January 2, 1791.

In the Symmes Purchase area, there were at least 37 privately built stockades. These posts were called stations and were usually named after a community leader. The stations featured a cluster of homes, the backs of which were connected by a picket wall. Residents of these stations requested and received federal troops for protection during this period. But the presence of a handful of soldiers was not enough to deter Indian attacks.

In January of 1792, Dunlop's Station near Cincinnati was attacked even though a Lieutenant Kingsbury and thirteen soldiers were on duty there. The

The Forts of Ohio

Indians captured a surveyor outside the gates and tortured him to death within earshot so his agonized screams could demoralize the garrison throughout the night.

Anthony Wayne was named commander of the American army in April of 1792 and he proceeded to recruit and drill a force that would be able to meet the Indian menace. But he initially trained his troops in the Pittsburgh area, leaving Wilkinson in command at Fort Washington.

The citizens of Cincinnati were generally a rowdy bunch, and the soldiers from the fort were easily led into temptation. To curb revelry among the troops, Wilkinson ordered that any soldier found drunk outside the fort's gates was to receive fifty lashes. In his zeal to obey this order, a young lieutenant named William Henry Harrison got into trouble.

Harrison had arrived at Fort Washington just after St. Clair's defeat. His father had signed the Declaration of Independence and now his father's friend George Washington had signed his new officer's commission. When the nineteen-year-old officer found an artificer of the garrison drunk he saw that he was given the prescribed punishment. However, artificers were skilled laborers such as blacksmiths who were sometimes enlisted men and sometimes private contractors. This one was a private citizen, who promptly hired the law firm of Blanchard and Smith to sue the government and got a judge to order Harrison's arrest, although he eventually escaped with only a reprimand.

There were more culturally uplifting activities

available, such as the theatrical performances that the troops sometimes took part in. And the Presbyterian Church that was organized in 1792 had both Wilkinson and Harrison as charter members. Wilkinson became a particularly prominent local citizen--he had a grand house built and was the owner of the first carriage in town. He also hosted lavish parties on his barge on the Ohio.

Wilkinson could afford to entertain so well because of the payments he regularly received from the Spanish. On one occasion, a $6,000 shipment of silver bound for him was lost when the Spanish envoys murdered their guide and absconded with the payment. They were caught but a judge and Wilkinson crony ruled their capture a military matter and removed them to the custody of the commander at Fort Washington. Thus, Wilkinson got custody of those who could expose him and hustled them out of the territory.

The Spanish hoped to gain western territory for themselves, or at least separate the western states from the rest of the United States. Wilkinson might have been more help to them in this goal had not Wayne been so effective. When Wayne moved his Legion to Cincinnati in 1793, he kept his men away from the temptations of the town. He chose a spot two miles downstream that he named Hobson's Choice.

Wayne's carefully trained troops succeeded where others had failed and after the Greeneville Treaty, there was no more Indian danger around Fort Washington. The fort was still used after the Indian Wars, although later the garrison consisted of just half of one company, or 35 men.

Young Lieutenant Harrison became commander of the fort in 1796, but he had larger goals in mind. He married Anna Symmes, the daughter of Judge Symmes, and resigned his commission to pursue a political career. However, he would return to Ohio forts on his route to the Presidency.

Fort Washington was abandoned in 1804, when the garrison was moved to the just finished Newport Barracks across the river in Kentucky. A large city grew on the site, and the fort's location was lost for a time. A monument was placed in Third Street near Broadway in 1902, and fifty years later, part of the powder magazine was unearthed in a construction project. Today, the marker has been moved to the former Guilford School on Fourth Street, near the Taft Museum.

The Forts of Ohio

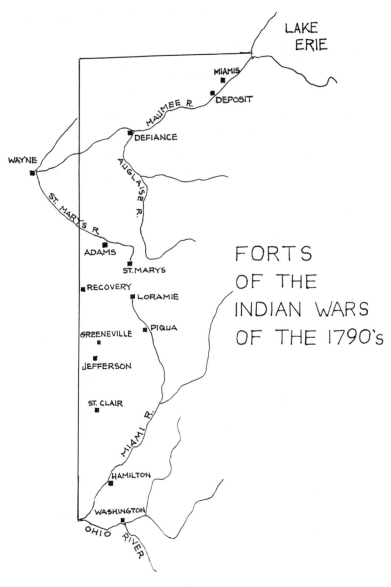

LAKE ERIE

MIAMIS

DEPOSIT

MAUMEE R.

DEFIANCE

WAYNE

AUGLAISE R.

ST. MARYS R.

ADAMS

ST. MARYS

FORTS
OF THE
INDIAN WARS
OF THE 1790's

RECOVERY

LORAMIE

GREENEVILLE

PIQUA

JEFFERSON

ST. CLAIR

MIAMI R.

HAMILTON

WASHINGTON

OHIO RIVER

The Forts of Ohio

FORTS OF THE INDIAN WARS OF THE 1790s

After the passage of the Ordinance of 1787 and the ratification of the Constitution, the drive towards Manifest Destiny could begin. But Ohio's role as the first state settled by free U.S. citizens was hindered by stiff resistance from unusually unified hostile Indians.

A tribal coalition soundly defeated two separate U.S. forces, and the few settlers remaining north of the Ohio had to huddle inside their community stockades. New settlement came to a standstill, and there was serious doubt that the infant nation would be able to expand at all.

The appointment of Anthony Wayne as General of the U.S. Army resulted in it no longer being necessary for pioneers to be "forting up". Working slowly and meticulously, Wayne trained an efficient army and built a string of supply forts that went to the heart of Indian country. In building these forts, Wayne avenged previous defeats, demoralized the Indians, and provided a strong enough supply system that he was able to defeat the unified Indians at the Battle of Fallen Timbers in 1794.

The next year Wayne was able to dictate peace terms that guaranteed the peaceful settlement of Ohio. Spain and England both acknowledged American sovereignty in the western country the same year in separate treaties and the Indians realized they were on their own in dealing with a new, young country that was capable of defending and expanding its borders

The Forts of Ohio

FORT HAMILTON

One of the many problems encountered by Harmar's 1790 expedition was the difficulty of supplying so large an army so far from their home base. It was acknowledged afterwards that a line of forts was needed to transport and protect supplies, and General Arthur St. Clair's army implemented this strategy in the fall of 1791. The first of these supply posts was Fort Hamilton, just twenty miles from Fort Washington. On September 11, St. Clair's slow moving army of 2,000 arrived at a fording place on the Miami River that featured a prairie of tall grass that could be used as forage for the army's animals. The fort on the east bank of the river was to be designed by Major William Ferguson, the artillery officer who had also worked on Fort Washington.

The reason that artillery officers were invariably chosen to design frontier forts was that they put the science into military science. Frontier armies tended to lack trained engineers, but artillery officers needed to have some scientific background to be able to operate their cannons properly. So those skilled in the science of destruction were also called upon as experts in constructing posts that would be difficult to destroy. Secretary of War Henry Knox had followed this route to a successful career, as the self taught former bookseller had been Washington's Chief of Artillery during the Revolution. Knox's most significant accomplishment during that war had been engineering the transfer of captured British cannon from Fort Ticonderoga to Boston, where their presence forced the British to evacuate. Ferguson was also a Revolutionary War veteran and a skilled and careful designer of forts. Unfortunately, he did not have long to enjoy the fruits of his labors, as he was killed in battle a month after Fort Hamilton was finished.

The new fort featured four blockhouses, barracks sufficient for 100 men, and several storehouses. The blockhouses were two stories and two of the bastions were equipped with artillery platforms. The outpost, which was named for Secretary of the Treasury Alexander Hamilton, featured a double row of pickets inside a drainage ditch, and St. Clair commented at length about the careful detail that went into its construction.

But this meticulous work took time, and the army stayed in place for two weeks while building the fort. It was late in the year and pressure was mounting for some sort of successful campaign, so it would have been preferable for an advance party to have built the fort earlier in the year. St. Clair was not on the site much of the time. He did not arrive until September 18, and left again October 2 to return to Fort Washington to bring back more militia.

By then the work was nearly done, and on October 3, the army moved out, leaving a garrison of around 100 who were all too ill or poorly supplied to proceed. The weather then turned bad and the army penetrated the deep woods for only 22 miles in the next five days. The garrison did not see the army again until November 6, when they returned with terrifying tales of a great defeat.

The Forts of Ohio

After James Wilkinson succeeded St. Clair as commander of the Ohio forts, Fort Hamilton was strengthened in March of 1792. Added were stables, a granary, artificers' yard, cistern and magazine to store gunpowder. Another improvement was a house built for Wilkinson's use that stood out among the plain pioneer architecture. It was a two story frame house with such civilized amenities as a cellar, wood floors, glass windows and plaster. The home also featured partitioned interiors and a two story veranda. It is no wonder that Wilkinson considered this fort his favorite.

Today the city of Hamilton surrounds the site, which is preserved in a small downtown park near the Main Street bridge. A plaque superimposes the fort's outline on the current city grid. Also on the site is the impressive 100 year old Soldiers, Sailors and Pioneers monument that can be seen from a great distance.

FORT JEFFERSON

For such a compact and isolated outpost, Fort Jefferson saw more than its share of suffering. It was the last fort built by a doomed army and the first returned to after a terrible defeat and as the most isolated fort was the site of numerous raids.

When St. Clair's army got to within six miles of the present site of Greenville in October 13, 1791, the General scouted for a fort site. The spot he chose was on a small knoll near a good spring next to a prairie suitable for grazing. Some criticized the location as being too low lying but a quick choice had to be made as it was late in the year and the army had traveled 44 miles since building the last supply post.

Construction began the next day under the direction of Major Ferguson, but the supply problems that had consistently plagued the army became an issue again. The army only had eighty axes and just one cross cut saw, so only 200 or so soldiers could be kept busy, while the remainder were idled for the next ten days. A lack of sufficient rations made it difficult to feed these non-working troops and then the weather got bad, which lowered morale even further. Four days of rain and hail began at the same time as construction and then a killer frost on October 21 eliminated forage for the livestock and horses. Also, many of the militia claimed that their period of enlistment was up and began to desert. Three of these men were caught and hanged before the army, but this failed to stem the exodus.

Despite these conditions, the fort was completed by October 23 and named for Secretary of State Thomas Jefferson. It was 114 feet square and similar in design to Fort Hamilton. There were ample barracks and storerooms and four bastions, with cannon mounted at the northeast and southwest corners. On the 24th the army moved out, leaving behind provisions and about 100 men too ill to travel, under the command of Captain Shaylor.

The army stumbled along into the late fall forest, their progress further hindered by the fact that St. Clair's gout had become so painful he often had to be carried in a litter. St. Clair hoped to discourage continued desertions by getting further from the safety of the American forts, heading into Indian country for exactly the wrong reasons. When some deserters were heard openly planning to loot an oncoming pack train, St. Clair sent 300 of his best troops back towards Fort Jefferson to escort the convoy. Consequently, the Americans' best regiment was not present when an Indian coalition surprised the army with an attack on November 4.

Although many of the Americans fought bravely

after the dawn attack began, the well organized Indian forces concentrated their fire on both officers and artillery men, and soon gained the upper hand. The U.S. Army had to retreat and the retreat became a rout as the panicked army streamed back towards Fort Jefferson. The army had only traveled 29 miles in the eleven days since leaving the fort; but, unencumbered by artillery, supplies, or even the muskets they threw down as they ran, the troops made the return trip in a single day.

As the terrified survivors regrouped at Fort Jefferson, they fully expected to be attacked. Since the fort was also low on provisions, St. Clair called a council and decided to continue the retreat that night. They left behind a token garrison and those that were too wounded to travel, many of whom soon died from lack of medical supplies and care. The Indians under Little Turtle and Blue Jacket did not follow up their victory, as many braves stopped to loot and to kill the wounded.

So Fort Jefferson was never directly attacked, but as the fort at the head of the line, it was the target of several smaller raids over the next year. Captain Shaylor's son was killed while on an unauthorized hunt in February of 1792. His successor as commander, a Captain Mumford, was killed a few hundred yards from the fort a few months later. On June 24, a fifteen man hay-cutting detachment was wiped out and in October a supply convoy was attacked between Forts Jefferson and St. Clair.

The army was determined to keep its most advanced post and made improvements. A couple of two-story blockhouses were added to guard a new corral and more ground was cleared around the fort. The most conspicuous improvement made under the administration of Wilkinson was another house for Wilkinson. The quarters he had made for his family here featured a large building with a sloping roof, dormers, and a cupola. The Wilkinsons hosted in their usual grand style here and on New Year's Day, 1794, they treated General Wayne to a dinner that featured such delicacies as mutton, plum pudding, and ice cream.

Wayne's building of Forts Greeneville and Recovery ended Fort Jefferson's role at the head of the line but it was still used as a supply post until it was abandoned and burned in the summer of 1796.

In 1907 the Greenville Historical Society erected a stone monument six feet square and 20 feet high at the site in the village of Fort Jefferson. In 1929 the site was purchased by the state for use as a park. The next year an archeological expedition from the Ohio State Historical Society discovered two tunnels--one leading to an underground powder magazine and the other to a nearby spring. Today a picnic shelter is also on the grounds of the four acre park, just off of State Route 121 in Darke County.

FORT ST. CLAIR

The 44-mile distance between Forts Hamilton and Jefferson created a logisitical supply problem, since pack train convoys generally covered only about 25 miles per day. A mid-point fort was needed to give any supply wagons a safe haven every night. James Wilkinson scouted for a suitable location in the winter of 1792 on his way to bury the victims of St. Clair's defeat. The spot chosen was near present day Eaton, where a good spring was the determining factor.

The main construction was completed in March, 1792 by a work crew of about 200 men led by militia Major John Gano. The chief carpenter for the project was John Thorp, who played this role in several other Ohio forts.

The Forts of Ohio

There was also a contingent of federal troops on hand, among them Ensign William Henry Harrison. The fort was 120 feet square with bastions on each corner. It was surrounded by 20 acres that had been burned out, and included a cattle pen. The fort's plain interior contained barracks, stables, storehouses, and a blacksmith shop.

The fort was named in honor of St. Clair, who kept his governor's job after resigning as Commander of the Army. Wilkinson claims that the fort was built in less than a week, but the militia is believed to have been on the site well before construction was complete in March. Wilkinson also boasted that his fort was sturdier than Forts Hamilton and Jefferson, and had been built quicker, cheaper, and with fewer men, although he offered no figures to substantiate this.

The fort was built with some trepidation. Harrison's duties included supervising a night guard without benefit of fires, which were prohibited for fear of attracting attack. But once completed, the fort stood unmolested throughout a relatively quiet summer. Part of the reason for this is that most Indians were meeting at the Grand Glaize in Defiance to discuss policy. Once the allied tribes had resolved to pursue a bellicose path, war parties were free to take up the hatchet in the fall.

A 200-warrior party under the leadership of Little Turtle was soon in the area. They discovered a pack train and tracked it to Fort St. Clair. The convoy was parked 200 yards outside the gates of the fort, guarded by a militia contingent under the command of Major John Adam. On the morning of November 6, 1792, the raiders attacked the convoy escort and sent them running to the fort. The Americans had six men killed, five wounded and four missing, while the Indians had two braves killed. The Indians briefly looted the convoy before the fort could react, but the biggest loss was the pack horses. Out of about 100 horses, only 23 were recovered. The boldness of this raid particularly upset Anthony Wayne, who was at that time under orders to avoid aggressive action.

Fort St. Clair continued to be used as a supply post during Wayne's Campaign. It was abandoned after the Greeneville Treaty and no drawing of the fort has been found.

Today the site, one mile from downtown Eaton in Preble County, is an 85 acre park maintained by the Ohio

The Forts of Ohio

Historical Society. In addition to picnic and other park activities are markers where the fort was located and under the nearby whispering pines to note where the victims of the wagon train attack fell.

The city of Eaton is named for a soldier who served in the Ohio forts of this era, but achieved fame elsewhere. William Eaton was an officer who actually served at Fort Recovery, where he impressed Anthony Wayne by making the effort to learn the Miami language. Eaton's facility with languages served him well as he learned Arabic and left the army for service in the Department of State. While stationed in North Africa in 1805 he led an odd conglomeration of soldiers across 600 miles of desert and captured two major Mediterranean ports. His success helped end a war with Barbary pirates who had been preying on American ships in the region.

FORT GREENE VILLE

Fort Greene Ville was really not a fort as much as it was a military city. In fact, it was more often referred to as Camp Greene Ville or just Greene Ville. But regardless of name, this post was large enough to host over 2,000 American troops and more than 1100 Indian guests, which made it the largest city for miles around.

Anthony Wayne had Fort Greene Ville built in 1793 as a winter quarters for his entire army. The new American commander had been recruiting and training his troops for over a year, and he wanted an advanced self-sufficient fort to launch a campaign from in the spring. Actually, Wayne was eager to fight before then if possible.

In the fall of 1793, Wayne's army was at Camp Hobson's Choice near Cincinnati, under orders to wait until the results of an Indian conference were known. When they received word that the Indians had rejected peace overtures, Wayne immediately ordered his army north on September 11. The army forged by Wayne was different than the one St. Clair led in the same direction two years earlier. This was a well-trained and streamlined force that traveled quickly and efficiently. Indian scouts following the army soon realized that they would not be able to surprise this force.

The Americans passed through Fort Jefferson on October 14, and advanced six miles farther north, where they found an excellent camp site. The spot featured a high level ground near a creek confluence on one side and overlooking a broad prairie on the other. St. Clair had camped on the spot after leaving Fort Jefferson, and would no doubt have used that spot for a fort had he seen it first.

Though Wayne wanted to attack, he did not want to rush into battle this late in the year, like St. Clair did. After a convoy train was attacked on October 17, Wayne decided to fortify his spot and use it as a springboard the next year.

Having to house the entire army required a stockade that was about 900 by 1,800 feet and covered over 50 acres of ground. Wayne ordered eight temporary buildings constructed to house troops during the building process. These buildings later were used as council houses during negotiations for the Greene Ville Treaty. The northern and western walls of the fort were irregularly shaped due to the proximity to a creek and the contours of the plateau the fort was built on.

The interior of the fort was designed as a military city sufficient to sustain over 2,000 men. The layout featured a city block- type setup. There were gardens, blacksmith shops, houses for both Generals Wayne and Wilkinson, even a slaughterhouse and tannery. On November 21, 1793, Wayne christened the new post Greene Ville, in honor of his Revolutionary comrade Nathaniel Greene.

By placing his army so far from organized settlements, Wayne faced problems in keeping his men provisioned. Wagon convoys needed to be well guarded and he had to keep an eye on his civilian contractors as well to prevent receiving rancid food and shoddy materials. One of his major contractors also carried on a secret correspondence with Wilkinson, inviting unsubstantiated suspicion of corruption.

The duplicitous Wilkinson was contemptuous of Wayne and helped polarize the ranks of the officers. As Wayne could be arbitrary and always was strict, it wasn't hard for the charming and loquacious Wilkinson to curry favor with dissatisfied officers. Morale was always a problem in confined quarters over long winters, but the situation was particularly pronounced at Greene Ville. One officer estimated that 15 duels were fought between officers in the first year of the fort's existence. These quarrels were frequently disastrous to both parties. In one duel, the loser died that day while the "winner" lingered in agony for a day and a half before dying.

Not all of the officers fought, however, as one of the most famous friendships in American history began at Fort Greene Ville. It was here that Meriwether Lewis met William Clark and started a partnership that would have great implications for the country. Clark was a veteran of the Fallen Timbers campaign when Lieutenant Lewis arrived at Greene Ville in 1795. The two had much in common as well-connected Virginia natives. Lewis was a protégé of his neighbor Thomas Jefferson and Clark was the brother of frontier hero George Rogers Clark. Both men left the service soon afterwards, but nearly a decade later when Jefferson asked Lewis to pick a partner for the momentous trip across the continent, he thought of his old army friend.

When spring finally arrived in 1794, Wayne wanted to take the offensive but felt he needed to strengthen his supply system and wait for reinforcements. On July 26, General Charles Scott arrived with 1,500 mounted Kentucky militia. Two days later, Wayne's army marched out of Greene Ville to inaugurate the campaign that culminated in the defeat of the Indians at Fallen Timbers. On November 2, the army returned in triumph to their winter quarters. They were greeted by a 24 gun salute from Greene Ville cannon.

The Indians were demoralized by Wayne's efficiency and began to think of negotiating for peace. When starving natives first approached the fort early in 1795,

The Forts of Ohio

Wayne made sure they saw how well-provisioned and strong the garrison was. The awed and hungry Indians spread the word and helped convince all tribes to sue for peace. Wayne announced a general peace conference for June 16, and by summer over 1,100 Indians from nearly all tribes had assembled at Greene Ville.

Many tribes were slow to arrive, so until business could formally begin, the Indians present were treated to entertainment that included a 4th of July fireworks show. Once negotiations began in earnest, however, it soon became apparent that the Americans now held the upper hand. Wayne was able to secure two thirds of what is now Ohio for settlement, as much any previous treaty had guaranteed. In addition, Wayne reserved the rights to his military forts that were at several key points in the heart of what was previously hostile Indian territory.

The Treaty of Greene Ville was signed on August 3, 1795. Among the American signers were Wayne, his aide-de-camp William Henry Harrison, and several translators and officials. Most major Indian chiefs signed, including Little Turtle of the Miami, Blue Jacket of the Shawnee, and Tarhe of the Wyandots. The Indians now realized that not only were the Americans a credible threat, but they were now left to deal with them on their own. The Greeneville Treaty marked the beginning of a 100-year period where Indian tribes steadily lost their lands to the Americans.

In that same year, the United States negotiated a treaty with Spain that allowed Americans use of the Mississippi to ship goods. And in Jay's Treaty with

England, the British finally agreed to evacuate Detroit and all other Great Lakes forts. These three treaties of 1795 removed all barriers to settlement and led to Ohio's attaining statehood just eight years later. None of them would have been possible without Wayne's military victory.

In December, Wayne returned to Philadelphia in triumph, but Wilkinson still plotted against him in his absence. When Wayne returned to Greene Ville in July of 1796, Wilkinson immediately asked permission to go to Philadelphia himself. To his Spanish paymasters in New Orleans he wrote, "I journey to Philadelphia to keep down the military establishment, to disgrace my commander, and to secure command of the army for myself." Though he was unable to detract from Wayne's success, Wilkinson did become commander of the U.S. Army when Wayne died on December 15, 1796. He continued both roles as commanding officer and Spanish spy for the next 16 years, and his treason was not discovered until the Spanish archives were opened long after his death.

With peace achieved, Fort Greene Ville was abandoned in 1796. The intensive construction throughout the fort made it a valuable source for wood and nails. Scavengers scoured the site for supplies that were used for new construction as far away as Dayton.

The site also was used again in 1805, when Tecumseh and his brother The Prophet located their village on the grounds. Tecumseh had boycotted the Greene Ville Treaty, but intentionally chose the site of the Indian subjugation there to build a village that would start an Indian unification movement. With Tecumseh providing political strength and The Prophet offering spiritual underpinnings to the movement, the success of the village alarmed nearby whites. Governor Thomas Kirker sent future governors Duncan MacArthur and Thomas Worthington to Greeneville in 1807 to discuss Indian intentions. Tecumseh accompanied them back to Chillicothe where he addressed the legislature and reassured them of his peaceful intentions. Shortly afterwards, the brothers moved to Indiana and continued their movement there.

After Tecumseh's death in battle in 1813, Greeneville again became the site of a major Indian treaty. In 1814, William Henry Harrison met representatives of all tribes here to negotiate a final peace. Throughout the proceedings, Harrison took great steps to insure that

everything mirrored as much as possible the events of the original treaty nearly twenty years before. Like Tecumseh and Wayne, he recognized the psychological advantages of sites, and he even wanted his headquarters on the exact spot where Wayne's had been.

Today, this special spot is covered by much of downtown Greenville. While markers such as the one in front of city hall are at certain locations, the exact site of the fort was unknown for a long time. However, in 2002 an archaeological expedition uncovered the site of one of the eight blockhouses that were later used as council houses. This discovery will make it easier to find the exact location of other parts of Ohio's largest fort.

FORT RECOVERY

Fort Recovery may have been in use for a short period of time, but the site was host to some of the fiercest and most significant fighting on the Ohio frontier. Built on the site of St. Clair's disastrous defeat of 1791, the fort lived up to its name with a victory over a large Indian army on June 30, 1794. This victory that came literally from the ashes of defeat helped make the ultimate victory at Fallen Timbers possible.

In late December of 1793, General Wilkinson invited Anthony Wayne to a Christmas dinner his wife was preparing at Fort Jefferson. Wayne declined and instead marched north from Fort Greeneville with eight companies of infantry on December 22. His goal was to recover the site of St. Clair's defeat, and build an advanced fort there. The spot was 23 miles north of Greeneville, approximately one day's journey for a pack train so it was a logical place for a new outpost. But Wayne also hoped to gain a psychological advantage by occupying the site of the Americans' greatest defeat.

It was a grim Christmas Eve for the troops, as they had to sweep the ground clear of the bones of their dead comrades before they could pitch their tents. On Christmas Day they buried those bones, which included around 500 skulls, and began building a new fort.

The artillery officer chosen to design the fort had been in that service as long as Secretary of War Knox. Major Henry Burbeck had served as an officer in his father's artillery regiment at the Battle of Bunker Hill. He remained in the army throughout the Revolution and rejoined in 1786 after three years as a civilian. He then was made commandant of the fort at West Point before being sent west as Wayne's chief of artillery. In this capacity he became the chief designer of Wayne's forts. Burbeck stayed in the army and finally attained the rank of General in the War of 1812.

No plat of the fort survives, but it was known to be a square design with four blockhouses that were twenty feet square. The fifteen-foot high stockade walls were built with sturdy timbers and the area around the fort was cleared for one thousand feet in all directions. Among the details of Burbeck's design were shutters on the musket portholes on the stockade wall that could be closed while the defenders were reloading.

Wayne was pleased with the results and wrote confidently that the new fort was "impervious to savage forces." While previous forts had been named for builders or government officials, Wayne wished to send a clear message with the name of his new advance post. Among the names he considered were Defiance and Restitution, but as the land had been recovered from the Indians, he decided to call it Fort Recovery.

Wayne and the bulk of his troops left on December 27, and Wayne did join the Wilkinsons for a New Year's Day feast at Fort Jefferson. Burbeck remained on the site for a few weeks supervising finishing touches and then a 200-man garrison was left under the command of Captain Alexander Gibson.

The energetic Gibson continued to make improvements on the fort. He added a second story to all the blockhouses and put cupolas on top to serve as lookout posts. The 36-foot-deep well in the fort produced water with a sulfurous taste, so Gibson had a tunnel built to the Wabash River. To store meat for the garrison, a twelve foot by fourteen foot ice house was built.

Fort Recovery also lived up to its name when the troops were able to recover most of the cannon that St. Clair's army had abandoned. Some of these field pieces had allegedly fallen into American hands at the surrender of Yorktown, but when the Indians recaptured them they had no way to transport them through the roadless wilderness.

The Forts of Ohio

They dismantled and hid the cannon, but the hiding places were betrayed by captives and the Americans were able to re-install them within the fort and fire a salute in celebration.

In the spring of 1794, Wayne was anxious to take the offensive, but he still was experiencing supply problems and the militia was late in gathering troops to supplement his army. While he was impatiently waiting, a large Indian army was coalescing with considerable help from the British. In June, a force of over 2,000 braves, larger than the army that had defeated St. Clair, began to move towards the Americans. This coalition included such prominent leaders as Little Turtle, Blue Jacket, the notorious renegade Simon Girty, and several British "observers". Their original goal was to strike deep into the American supply route, but they changed this when they heard of a large supply convoy en route to Fort Recovery.

On the evening of June 29, 1794, a large pack train under the command of Major William McMahon arrived at the fort. The convoy had 360 horses hauling 1,200 kegs of flour and was escorted by 140 troops that included 50 mounted dragoons. Too large to fit inside the fort, the convoy spent the night outside the gates. The next morning, they began the return trip but had just started when they were ambushed by the full force of the Indians.

The soldiers panicked and ran, and the officers who tried to rally them were the first to be picked off, including McMahon, who, at six foot six, presented an easy target. As the troops streamed towards the protection of the fort, the Indians drove off the cattle and horses. But rather than loot the pack trains, the attackers impulsively attacked the fort directly.

It was rare for Indians to storm a stockade, but this was an overconfident and unusually large force. But the Indians' charge at the pickets was the high water mark of their confederacy. Gibson was ready for them and the fort's defenses worked as designed, with a telling fire coming through the loopholes in the stockade. The recovered artillery also frustrated the invaders, who had hoped to use the same cannon against the fort. Though outnumbered ten to one, the garrison easily repulsed the Indians and inflicted heavy losses. Another attack was attempted on the morning of July 1, but was treated similarly and the Indians withdrew.

The American losses in this battle were high-22 dead and 30 wounded, but Wayne was exultant that the Indians had been beaten "with loss and disgrace from that very field where they had upon a former occasion been proudly victorious." The victory at Fort Recovery also made the job easier for the rest of Wayne's army. After capturing the pack train, many Indians had gotten their fill of blood and plunder, and after an unsuccessful attack they had gotten their fill of defeat. Their grand coalition began to break up as many of the Chippewa and Ottawa and northern Great Lakes warriors began to leave for home. These defections meant that Wayne had a significantly smaller force opposing him at Fallen Timbers.

The Forts of Ohio

The action at the site of Fort Recovery perfectly illustrates the dynamics of frontier fort warfare. On open ground the Indians were formidable, which is why they usually attacked convoys rather than forts. Even a large army like St. Clair's was not safe from surprise attack and annihilation. But once the soldiers were safely inside a fort, the odds changed considerably. A well designed fort was virtually impregnable and Indians rarely even considered an open attack. Outside of treachery or an unlikely prolonged siege, the only thing that could bring down a fort was artillery.

The presence of cannons shifted the dynamics again, as frontier forts were rarely strong enough to hold up to cannonballs. When the British hauled cannon to Kentucky during the Revolution, the garrison at Ruddle's Station surrendered without a fight. But the problem with artillery was transporting them through the roadless swamps and forests. The Indians also lacked the ability to fire them, although British officers at Fort Recovery might have overcome this had they had the opportunity. But the Americans held both the fort and the artillery, so they were able to hold off one of the largest Indian armies ever assembled and guarantee that Fort Recovery would live up to its name.

The fort was abandoned after the Greeneville Treaty but today it is a featured site of the Ohio Historical Society. In addition to a museum, a single stockade wall and blockhouses have been rebuilt.

FORT ADAMS

One of the smallest of the Ohio forts, Fort Adams is known chiefly because the army's commanding general was nearly killed here during the four day period when the fort was being constructed.

After leaving Fort Greeneville in July 1794, Anthony Wayne's 3,500-man-army advanced slowly but confidently. The troops only averaged about twelve miles a day, but they carefully fortified each camp site and made surprise attacks impossible. On the evening of August 1,

The Forts of Ohio

1794, Wayne's American Legion arrived at the banks of the St. Marys River, ten miles north of present-day Celina. Here Wayne decided to build a supply post on the south bank of the river.

The site was significant because the troops were now in the Lake Erie watershed. The St. Marys flowed northwest to present-day Fort Wayne, then formed the Maumee, which flowed northeast to the western end of Lake Erie. The Americans could now advance on the Maumee Rapids by either a land or water route.

But the actual site of the new fort left much to be desired. It was low-lying, marshy, and easily flooded. The building crew also had to deal with intensive August heat and mosquitoes, while the portion of the army not actively engaged in construction was able to go swimming and fishing. The new fort, which Wayne named for Vice President John Adams, had stockade walls that were only 24 feet long. There were two eighteen-foot-square blockhouses on opposite corners. Inside were two buildings with hipped roofs: a commandant's quarters and a guard house.

On the afternoon of August 3, Wayne left his supervisory duties to avoid the heat with a nap in his tent. Shortly after 3 o'clock, a large beech tree suddenly fell on his tent and smashed it. The only thing that kept Wayne from being, as he said, "crushed to atoms", was that the tree landed on top of a stump just inches from Wayne's head. Wayne was thus miraculously only bruised, although he was obviously quite shaken. At the time it was considered a fluke accident, but Wayne gradually came to feel that the incident was "probably premeditated" with an implied suspicion that Wilkinson was behind it.

There was no actual evidence to support this, just as there was no evidence of Wilkinson's rumored activities with Spain found during his lifetime. But he would have been capable of such a scheme, and at least one contemporary historian believes Wilkinson may have ordered the murder of Meriwether Lewis. In 1809 Lewis had succeeded Wilkinson as governor of Louisiana Territory after Wilkinson's involvement with Aaron Burr's plans became public. On his way to Washington, the troubled Lewis died mysteriously of a gunshot wound. The death was ruled a suicide, but since Lewis may have discovered evidence of extensive fraudulent activity during his predecessor's term, Wilkinson would have had a motive for murder, and Lewis' trip gave him opportunity.

On the evening of August 3, the army was reinforced by a contingent of Kentucky militia bearing additional supplies, and Wayne decided to move on. He left behind a detail of 40 men too ill to travel under the command of Captain James Underhill to finish the fort. Underhill felt he was being abandoned, especially since Indians were known to visit military campsites right after they were vacated. His small crew of invalids also had a lot of work to do, as the blockhouses still had no roofs, the gates were not yet hung and much of the timber was still across the river, which was 50 yards wide.

The Forts of Ohio

The fort was completed without incident, however, as the Indians were apparently too busy dealing with the rest of the army. Nothing of significance happened during the rest of Fort Adams' brief history, but it did mark the beginning of Wayne's dependence on water routes for his supply lines. There is no trace of Fort Adams today.

FORT DEFIANCE

Even more than its taunting name, it was the location of Fort Defiance that had a demoralizing effect on the Indian coalition. By erecting a sturdy fort in the middle of the Indians' most cultivated lands, Anthony Wayne showed that his American Legion was a force to be reckoned with.

The area at the confluence of the Auglaize and Maumee Rivers had been important to the Indians as far back as the early 1700's, when the French had a presence there. Located at the edge of the great Black Swamp and between the Maumee Rapids and the confluence of the St. Joseph and St. Marys Rivers, the Grand Glaize, as the area was called, was a natural gathering point with its fertile fields.

By the 1790s, the area was home to the villages of major chiefs of several tribes of the Indian coalition. Little Turtle of the Miami, Blue Jacket of the Shawnee and Buckongahelas of the Delaware all lived nearby. Right at the confluence of the Auglaize and Maumee was where

British agents Elliot, McKee and Simon Girty had set up a trading post.

In 1792, the confluence hosted the largest concentration of Native Americans assembled in one spot up to that time. Over 4,000 gathered in September of that year to reaffirm their insistence on the Ohio River as the boundary limit for white settlement. But now Anthony Wayne was threatening the strength of that alliance by marching into Indian country.

As Wayne's legion left Fort Adams on August 4, 1794, the Indians had to abandon their Grand Glaize villages in the face of the advancing army. When they entered the area on August 7, the Americans were astounded at the extent of what seemed almost one continuous village to them. After traveling through dense forests, future explorer William Clark was surprised to find "a handsome view up and down the rivers, the margins of which are covered with the most luxuriant growths of corn", interspersed with "almost every species of proticultural vegetables in the greatest abundance."

Wayne considered the Grand Glaize to be "the grand emporium of the hostile Indians of the West" and he sought to neutralize the area by erecting a strong post on the spot. His army spent a week at the confluence, defiantly building a fort at the strongest point of Indian power and British influence. Under the supervision of Henry Burbeck, the army built a square fort with 60- foot curtains and 22-foot- square blockhouses at each bastion. The timbers used for pickets had to be at least twelve inches in diameter and fifteen feet long and were sunk three feet into the ground. With all federal troops engaged in construction, the fort was completed by August 15, complete with fireplaces and chimneys in each blockhouse. Wayne was so satisfied with the post's sturdiness that he could "defy all the devils in Hell to take it" and he named it Fort Defiance.

During this period, Wayne was also engaged in some last-minute negotiating. He wrote to the Indians and issued this prophetic warning about British support: "Brothers, be no longer deceived or led astray by the false promises and language of the bad men at the foot of the rapids; they have neither the power nor the inclination to protect you." The Indians asked for a ten-day delay to consider Wayne's message. Rather than give the enemy time to gather, Wayne ignored their request and crossed the Maumee and headed towards the rapids, leaving 90 men under Major Thomas Hunt to defend Fort Defiance. Hunt was an experienced officer with a long-term association with Wayne. He had been a Minute Man at Lexington and Concord, and was wounded at Yorktown and during Wayne's successful raid on Stony Point.

After defeating the Indians at Fallen Timbers on August 20, Wayne was able to see first hand how strong the British Fort Miamis was. When the army returned to Fort Defiance on August 23, he decided to further strengthen the fort so that it could withstand an assault by British artillery. This entailed reinforcing the walls with another row of pickets and digging a deep parapet trench around the fort. At the south gate this trench was crossed by an elaborate pulley-drawn drawbridge. Officers' quarters and storehouses were also added and a covered trench dug down to the river.

After being resupplied by a convoy on September 10, Wayne left 200 men under Hunt and took the rest of his army upstream on the Maumee where they built Fort Wayne on the spot that was the other major location of Indian cooperation. As part of the terms of the Greeneville Treaty, Wayne insisted that Forts Defiance and Wayne remain under U.S. control, even though they were on the Indian side of the negotiated boundary.

The British Lieutenant Governor of Canada, John Simcoe, was said to have wanted to attack Fort Defiance just because of its name. But England was not about to commit to another foreign war and no attack was forthcoming. As the most advanced American fort, Defiance was where Indians first went to seek peace, and increasing numbers of them did so. After the Greeneville Treaty, the size of the garrison was reduced to 56 men early in 1796. The fort was abandoned in June of that year when the garrison moved to Fort Miamis when the British evacuated that post. On the spot today is the Defiance Public Library and a small city park overlooking the still scenic confluence.

FORT DEPOSIT

Fort Deposit was the shortest lived of the Ohio forts, having been only briefly needed for one of its major functions and not needed at all for its other one. Built right before the Battle of Fallen Timbers, it was one more illustration of the difference between Wayne's and St. Clair's campaigns.

Wayne was aware of how much equipment and supplies had been abandoned to the Indians at St. Clair's defeat. With battle imminent, Wayne ordered all excess baggage to be deposited before the army was engaged. A stripped down army was a more efficient one, and the added purpose was to have a fortified camp to retreat towards if the battle went poorly, since the Americans had run nearly 30 miles to Fort Jefferson after St. Clair's Defeat.

The temporary structure called Fort Deposit was built on the north bank of the Maumee near present-day

Waterville on August 19, 1794. Wayne's campsites were known for careful attention to security, and this camp was even more fortified than most. There were three bastions surrounded by breastworks seven feet high. When the army left for battle the next day, the post was left under the command of Captain Zebulon Pike. Pike was a Revolutionary War veteran and the father of Zebulon Montgomery Pike, whose own military career would take him west, where he discovered Pike's Peak in 1806.

Halting their advance to construct Fort Deposit helped contribute to the ultimate American victory. Indians traditionally fasted before they went into battle, a practice which had medical as well as spiritual advantages, as in the event of stomach wounds there was less chance of fatal infection. They had already picked out a stand of timber felled by a tornado where they would do battle, and they expected the Americans to be there on the 19th. But when Wayne stopped to deposit his baggage, the Indians were forced to fast for an additional day and consequently were not in top shape to do battle.

Since Fallen Timbers was an American victory, Fort Deposit was not needed as a rallying point and the post was abandoned after the army had retrieved its baggage. No trace of the fort remains today.

The Forts of Ohio

FORT MIAMIS

Fort Miamis was the second and last fort built by the British in what eventually became Ohio. Like its predecessor, Fort Sandusky, the building of Fort Miamis was a blatant violation of international treaty. But while Fort Sandusky was noted for being the only Ohio fort to be captured and destroyed, Fort Miamis became known because of a battle that did not take place on its site.

The Maumee River, also called the Miami of the Lakes, had always been important to Indian trade. The French built a fort called Fort Miami at the beginning of the river (present day Fort Wayne) in 1680. The Maumee was navigable to Great Lakes ships from its mouth to the edge of the rapids found between present-day Perrysburg and Maumee. British trader Alexander McKee had a post here on an island in the river, and the area became a center of British influence in the early 1790s.

According to the terms of the Treaty of Paris of 1783, the British were to recognize American independence and withdraw from their forts on the American side of the Great Lakes. However, they were reluctant to give up their lucrative fur trade and influence with the Indians. They also refused to surrender these parts on the grounds that America had voided the treaty by refusing to compensate Loyalists for confiscated property.

The Indians needed British support and supplies if they were to resist American encroachment. But British officials had to be careful not to go too far in their promises since they were already in an expensive war with revolutionary France. Yet early in 1794, the British governor of Canada announced that he expected England would be at war with the United States soon, and Indian hopes of a military alliance rose. But the British had talked tough in the past, and many Indians were skeptical without any sign of action.

They got this in April of 1794 when Canadian Lieutenant Governor John Simcoe arrived on the north bank of the Maumee Rapids to select a site for a new fort. Also sent from Detroit were 120 soldiers from the 24th Regiment and a detachment of Royal Artillery. Supplies and cannon were sent from Detroit on the ships *Brazen* and *Spitfire*, and the British also planned to build a supply station on Turtle Island at the mouth of the Maumee Bay.

The work was supervised by Lieutenant Robert Pilkington of the Royal Engineers, who had been trained in fort design. The post, which was called Fort Miamis, was on an elevated parapet of earth and surrounded by a ditch. The stockade walls were 20 feet high and made with timbers that were 12 inches thick. The fort was well-equppied with cannon, having four pieces that fired nine pound cannonballs, four that shot six pound balls, and six smaller howitzers. The garrison under Major William Campbell numbered between 180 and 250 men.

Work proceeded slowly, but by August, Simcoe was able to report that they were in "a complete state of defiance". The British saw this new fort as an extension of their fur trade, while the Indians saw it as a sure sign the redcoats planned to go to war alongside them. The Americans saw this new construction on land ceded to the U.S. an outrage that could lead to war with England.

It was no coincidence that the Indians chose to fight Wayne's army within a few miles of Fort Miamis. There were no British soldiers at the Battle of Fallen Timbers, but there was a contingent of Canadian militia serving with the Indians. The tribal leaders expected to be able to retreat to the fort if needed, and they were shocked to find the gates barred after the battle. Campbell reportedly told them "you are painted [for war] too much, my children, and I can't let you in."

With the fleeing Indians in disarray, Wayne's army marched to within a mile of the fort and camped for the night. With American and British troops so close together, there was a very real possibility of an international war being launched from an isolated Ohio outpost. There was a precedent for such an occurrence. In 1754, a young Virginia militia officer named George Washington had attacked French troops in western Pennsylvania. A larger French force chased Washington and forced him to surrender at Fort Necessity, and the incident started the Seven Years' War that soon engulfed all of Europe. The British were able to take all of Canada as a result of that war, but there were several costly defeats before they were able to prevail.

Wayne had almost been passed over as a commander of the American army because Washington was worried that Mad Anthony was too impetuous for so delicate a mission. But it is worth noting that Wayne did not repeat his Commander-in-chief's mistake of forty years before and start a war that his country was not ready for.

But he did come close to the brink. On the morning of August 21, Campbell sent a message to Wayne demanding, "In what light am I to view your making such near approaches to this garrison?" Wayne replied that Fort Miamis was on American soil and should be evacuated, but Campbell responded that he would not abandon his post without orders from his supervisors. The increasingly testy exchange of letters between the two commanders led Wayne into seriously considering an assault on the fort. He resolved to make a final insulting reconnoiter first.

On the morning of August 22, the American commander emerged on horseback, alone, into the clearing around the fort. Wayne then rode to within pistol range of the fort and slowly rode around the entire perimeter, making note of the fort's defenses. According to one account, he hurled insults at the garrison, but his presence was insult enough. The outraged British could not risk war by shooting the opposing commander, and the Indians who were watching became even more impressed by Wayne's bravery and boldness.

Wayne now realized that the fort could not be taken without suffering heavy losses. He also knew that he would no longer have to risk a war to show the Indians the hollowness of British professions of support. While the British garrison slept beside their loaded cannons at night, Wayne decided to return to Fort Deposit on August 23.

The Forts of Ohio

But first he ordered everything around the fort to be destroyed. All Indian homes and crops and McKee's trading post were burned and Wayne noted with satisfaction that "a numberous garrison well supplied with artillery have been compelled to remain tacit spectators of the general conflagration around them." The Americans then conducted a funeral service for their dead that included a sixteen gun salute and then returned to their own forts.

Wayne's actions had dealt a crippling blow to British credibility, and he had enhanced his own mystique to where the awed Indians began to feel they might be better off negotiating with him. At the same time, John Jay was in London working on a treaty that would result in a British evacuation of the contested forts at Detroit, Niagara, and Michilimackinac. In July of 1796 the British turned Fort Miamis over to the Americans from Fort Defiance, and the next month Detroit was finally evacuated.

Although never again would a foreign power build a fort in Ohio, the site of Fort Miamis would play a role in one more invasion. In 1813, the British and Indians laid siege to Fort Meigs on the other side of the Maumee. An American force coming to relieve the garrison was lured into an ambush, with many of them then taken captive by the Indians. These prisoners were taken to the abandoned site of Fort Miamis, where the Indians began to systematically massacre them.

The executions were ended when Tecumseh suddenly appeared on the scene. Tecumseh was known for his opposition to torture and execution of helpless captives, an unusual stance for an Indian. He quickly and loudly demanded the killing be stopped and berated British officers present for permitting the killing to proceed unchecked. Tecumseh's dramatic rescue of American soldiers was one of the last military actions at any Ohio fort.

Today the scene of all this drama is a park maintained by the city of Maumee along River Road.

FORT PIQUA

The fort that stood on this site in 1795 and 1796 was of little significance, but the site itself was a crucial location that spanned the entire era of Indian and white relations in Ohio. The spot where Loramie Creek meets the

The Forts of Ohio

Miami River was an important part of a well-traveled water route between Lake Erie and the Ohio River and hosted lots of action.

As early as 1747 the site was occupied by a village under the leadership of a Miami chief who was called Old Britain because of his preference to the English and their trade goods. While most Indians had aligned themselves with the French traders, Old Britain welcomed British traders and their cheaper goods to his village. The British traders even built a palisade around their compound which was called Fort Pickawillany.

Although this post was a private commercial venture and not a military fort, the French were nonetheless alarmed. In 1749 they sent a military force under Celeron de Bieneville that claimed jurisdiction of all the Ohio country by the French. This group left lead plates claiming ownership at major stream confluences, and at Pickawillany they also warned Old Britain. These warnings were ignored and when frontiersman Christopher Gist visited Pickawillany in 1750, he wrote about the post in the first account of the Ohio country written in English.

On June 21, 1752, Pickawillany was attacked by a French led force of northern lakes Indians. The fort surrendered, one trader was killed, and the victors then boiled and ate Old Britain. This ended British trade in the region for a while, but in the war that this incident helped start, England was able to capture all of France's holdings in North America.

The Forts of Ohio

During the American Revolution, raiding parties from the Detroit area passed through on their way to Kentucky. Their preferred route was to go upstream on the St. Mary's River, portage to Loramie Creek and go downstream to the Great Miami. American counter raids from Kentucky tended to use the same route in reverse. After the war, General Harmar's army came through the area, but it wasn't until after the Battle of Fallen Timbers that Anthony Wayne decided to use this water route as his main supply line.

Wayne's biggest problem was safely transporting supplies, as it was convoys rather than his forts that came under attack. An almost all water route was decided upon, which could transport supplies more efficiently and safely. Wayne's army stopped here in October of 1794 while returning to Fort Greeneville, but a fort was not built here until the following fall as Wayne did not want to stir up Indian unrest with new fort construction until after he negotiated a treaty.

However, Wayne did correspond with his chief fort designer Henry Burbeck about a series of these forts to handle the transfer of supplies over the portage from Ohio to Lake Erie watersheds. Fort Piqua, the first of this chain, was constructed not far from the old site of Pickawillany in October 1795. Little is known of the fort or garrison, but since the commanding officer George Salmon, only held the rank of Ensign, it was most likely a small post, although a Captain L.N. Vischer was later the commander. Supplies arriving here were sent upstream fourteen miles to Fort

The Forts of Ohio

Loramie in higher water and transferred by land in low water. After Detroit was surrendered to the Americans in 1796 the fort was no longer needed and was abandoned.

But the site of Fort Piqua was significant because of the effect it had on one of Wayne's wagon drivers. The first time that teamster John Johnston saw this spot he was so impressed by it that he decided it would be his future home if at all possible. The teenaged Irish immigrant saw excellent farm land, a good location for a house, and "an unusually large and never failing spring of the purest and coldest water."

After working in the mercantile business for a few years, Johnston became the factor of the Indian agency at Fort Wayne in 1802. The federal government controlled all trade with Indians to better control them as well as protect them from unscrupulous traders and the temptations of alcohol. The factor was essentially the business manager for the Indian stores or factory, while the Indian agent was responsible for policy. Johnston scrupulously tried to help the Indians better their lot, but clashed with Indian agent William Wells, whom he called "too unprincipled to be employed anywhere." Johnston eventually resigned from the agency in 1811 when he was able to purchase his dream home site and move to Piqua.

He began to build his impressive three-story brick farmhouse on the property soon afterwards, but his skills in dealing with Native Americans were soon needed by the government. When the War of 1812 began, the frontier was thrown into turmoil as many Indians joined the British.

However, many others were neutral or pro-American and persuasion was needed to keep them that way. Johnston was appointed agent to deal with the Shawnee tribe, and because of his good reputation, other tribes asked to deal with him.

In September of 1812, Johnston's Piqua farm was host to a conference of over 3,000 Indians not long after Detroit had been surrendered to the British. Many Indians stayed together in this area afterwards, and Indians soon outnumbered whites in the Piqua area. This alarmed the settlers, and the Indians feared attacks from whites who made no effort to distinguish between good and bad Indians. While working closely with American commander William Henry Harrison, Johnston realized that having the pro-American Indians and the Americans in one place was "the best protection to this frontier", and through his skills was able to maintain a peaceful climate throughout the war.

After the war, Johnston continued as Indian agent from his farm. His wife was a Quaker, and through her he recruited Quaker missionaries to teach the Indians agriculture and other ways of the whites so they might adapt and survive. When an effort was made to split his agency, the Ohio tribes unanimously requested Johnston retain full control, saying "we are confident he is our real friend." So great was Johnston's integrity and ability that in 1824 he was able to get conviction and execution of a group of whites who had murdered some Indians--an example of justice that was rare on the frontier.

The Forts of Ohio

The election of Andrew Jackson as president led to a change of all federal office holders, and Johnston was replaced in 1830. He continued to work his farm and also was active in the community. He served on the state canal commission, was a trustee for Miami University, and was president of the Ohio Historical and Philosophical Society.

The Ohio Indians meanwhile were gradually selling their lands and allowing themselves to be removed to the western U.S. By the 1840s only the Wyandot tribe remained, and in 1841 the 66-year-old Johnston was named to negotiate a treaty to purchase this remaining reservation. His appointment came from his old friend Harrison, who had recently been elected President. He died just six weeks after his inauguration, and nine days after appointing Johnston.

Johnston successfully negotiated a treaty that was signed at Upper Sandusky on March 17, 1843. Just a few days later, Charles Dickens arrived at the same inn on his American tour. Dickens, in his American Notes, called Johnston "a mild old gentleman" who "gave me a very moving account of their [the Wyandots] strong attachments to the familiar scenes of their infancy... He had witnessed many such removals, and always with pain, though he knew they departed for their own good."

When Johnston returned to his Piqua farm, the transformation was complete. One hundred years earlier the area around his home had never seen an English-speaking white man. Fifty years earlier, he and Harrison, and others were trying to claim an area that the Indians still had a hold on. And now Ohio was a bustling state with canals and railroads and visiting English authors, and the last of the Indians were gone.

Today the scene of all this drama is the site of the Piqua Historical Area, a Gateway site of the Ohio Historical Society. This 175 acre park includes the sites of Pickawillany and Fort Piqua as well as Johnston's original farmhouse. The farm features demonstrators who show how life was in Johnston's time. Also on the site is a museum that stresses Native American life in Ohio. A replica canal boat, the General Harrison, takes tourists for a ride on the water, and the Buckeye Trail goes along the waterway north for three miles to Lockington Locks. The Piqua Historical Area is three miles northwest of Piqua on State Route 66 in Shelby County.

The Forts of Ohio

FORT LORAMIE

Fort Loramie was the middle of the three supply portage posts built by Anthony Wayne. Like the others, it was built in a location that had already been deemed useful. There had been a trading post at the head of navigation on Loramie Creek as early as 1769. In that year the French Canadian, Peter Loramie, set up a trading post there. Loramie was apparently a Jesuit priest, but his store was a decidedly secular venture. Though Canada was now under British control, the original French settlers were generally loyal to their new country once they were granted freedom to practice their religion.

Loramie's store prospered on its location between the Ohio River and Lake Erie watersheds. During the Revolution, British and Indian raiding parties got their supplies here on their way to attack Kentucky settlements. This incensed the Kentuckians, and in November of 1782, George Rogers Clark led a raid and destroyed Loramie's Store. Loramie and most of his partners escaped but the store was not rebuilt.

When Anthony Wayne decided to utilize a water based supply route, he picked the route that had already been used. This meant the site of Loramie's Store was an ideal location for a post. At a spot just north of the present Miami County village of Fort Loramie was a good spring located at the head of high water navigation. From here, boats could be unloaded onto wagons for a short portage to the St. Mary's River.

91

Wayne was proud to point out that now "the whole of the land transport from Pittsburgh to Detroit is but eleven miles", with all other travel being by water. While the location of the fort is known, the size or number of the garrison is not. Burbeck designed the fort and the commander was Edward Butler, who was stationed here but also had authority over Forts Piqua and St. Mary's. Butler was the son of General Richard Butler, the negotiator of the Treaty of Fort Finney, who was killed while second-in-command at St. Clair's Defeat. The elder Butler had also been a friend of Wayne's during the Revolution.

Fort Loramie was completed in November of 1795, and during the next year work was done on building a road to Fort St. Mary's. But when Detroit was turned over to the Americans in July, 1796, there was no more need for these supply forts and they were abandoned. The fort was used again as a way-station during the War of 1812. Today there is a marker on Route 66 just north of the village of Fort Loramie to denote the location of the fort.

FORT ST. MARYS

The northernmost post on Anthony Wayne's water-based supply route was also selected because the site had been used previously. The current site of the Auglaize County town of St. Marys had been a trading post and village headed by James Girty, a brother of the notorious renegade, Simon Girty. James had been a partner of Peter Loramie, and had fled to the banks of the St. Mary's River after George Roger Clark's men had destroyed Loramie's Store in 1782.

From 1783 to 1790, Girty maintained his trading post. He was married to a Shawnee woman, but the village around his post that came to be called Girty's Town was home to members of assorted tribes. Within his palisaded post, Girty traded for furs which he sent up the Maumee Rivers to Detroit. He also served as an unofficial representative of the British, so when Harmar's army approached in 1790, he fled the area.

When Wayne had Fort St. Marys built on the site in 1795, many referred to it as Fort Girty Town. Fort names were sometimes a generation behind in St. Marys, because when Fort Barbee was built during the War of 1812, many referred to that post as Fort St. Marys.

The Forts of Ohio

Wayne had considered a water route for supplies during the summer of 1794, but it wasn't until a year later that he authorized Henry Burbeck to build a blockhouse to store building supplies at St. Marys. The actual construction of the fort was done in October, 1795, by a detail under the command of Lieutenant John Michael. After the small fort was completed, the officer in charge was Lieutenant John Whistler. Whistler had come to America with the British Army during the Revolution and was captured when Burgoyne surrendered at Saratoga. He returned to this country and took up a military career, as did his son. His grandson, however, took a different path as the painter, James Abbot McNeil Whistler.

As the first fort on the Lake Erie watershed, Fort St. Marys was where the military stores were transferred from wagons to boats. A crude road was built between Forts Loramie and St. Marys, and at St. Marys boat building became a major activity. Once the new boats were launched they could float to Fort Wayne in seven days in moderate waters, although they tied up at night. At low water, navigation was more difficult, but the issue became moot after the fall of Detroit in 1796.

The fort was abandoned in 1796. When a new fort was built in 1812, it was located slightly closer to downtown St. Marys, almost adjacent to the old grounds. There is a marker in the Lutheran Cemetery noting the location of Fort St. Marys and an archaeological dig has uncovered several artifacts from the era.

The Forts of Ohio

FORT INDUSTRY

Fort Industry is Ohio's mystery fort. Its existence is confirmed by the Treaty of Fort Industry that was signed on July 4, 1805, and its location was known to be where Swan Creek meets the Maumee River. This puts the fort in present-day downtown Toledo, near the junction of Summit and Monroe Streets.

But there is considerable uncertainty about who built the fort and when. It was said that General Wayne had it built right after the Battle of Fallen Timbers, and given Wayne's tendency to name forts after attributes, this sounds plausible. But this would have put an American fort between the British fort Miamis and Detroit, and Wayne had a hard enough time defending and supplying his forts that were contiguous. Also, other accounts mention the Swan Creek area as being a gathering place for disgruntled Indians after Fallen Timbers, and there are no references to a fort here by Wayne or any of his officers.

In fact, there are almost no references to Fort Industry in official U.S. documents at any time except for when the U.S. and Indians signed a treaty there. It is most likely that Fort Industry, like Fort Finney, was constructed solely for the purpose of conducting an Indian treaty. If so, it would have been built and temporarily manned by Federal troops, although it is not known how many or who the commanding officer was.

The purpose of the treaty was to purchase more Indian land. The part of Ohio that was ceded here was the western extension of the Western Reserve called the Firelands. This land was so named because it was awarded to compensate Connecticut residents whose homes had been burned during the Revolution. Other lands were being sold at this time in what was to become Indiana and Michigan. Any treaty required the pomp and pageantry of a fort, particularly one to be signed of the 4th of July.

There is no reference made to Fort Industry after the signing of this treaty so it was most likely abandoned immediately afterwards. There is no trace of the fort remaining in the busy setting on the site today.

The Forts of Ohio

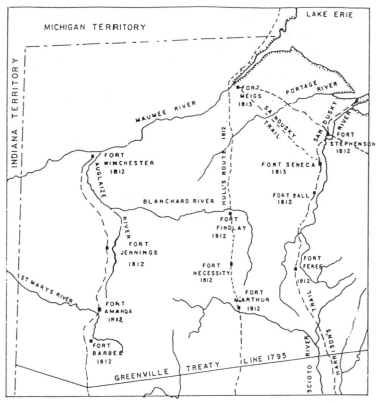

FORTS OF THE WAR OF 1812

The Forts of Ohio

FORTS OF THE WAR OF 1812

After nearly twenty years of peace, there was one more episode of war in frontier Ohio. The War of 1812 represented the last chance for England to check American expansion, and for an Indian buffer state to exist between the U.S and Canada.

Although the western states were eager for war, they were not prepared for it and suffered some early disasters. The first army to pass through Ohio surrendered without a fight and the second fell victim to a massacre. But under the leadership of William Henry Harrison, the Americans rallied and not only expelled British and Indian forces from the state, but launched a successful invasion of Canada.

In the initial panic after early defeats there were numerous blockhouses and local militia stockades built for defense. Of these approximately fifty-five locations, only a dozen were built as a part of an overall military campaign. Many of these forts were used only as supply depots, but a few were the scenes of high drama and heated battles. All of the forts of this era were built within a thirteen month period, and are presented here in geographic rather than chronological order.

After Commodore Perry's victory on Lake Erie cleared the way for the land troops, this last threat to Ohio was over. No longer could ships from the British Navy shell the future suburbs of Toledo, and there would be no more Indian attacks on Ohio forts or citizens.

The Forts of Ohio

FORT MCARTHUR

The Treaty of Greeneville guaranteed peaceful settlement of much of Ohio, but could not provide permanent peace on the frontier. Whites and Indians lived close to each other for eighteen years, but there was always an undercurrent of tension. Tecumseh and his brother, The Prophet, posed the biggest threat to whites because they preached Indian unity. Their insistence that all tribes negotiate as one alarmed Americans as much as the threat of British support for Indian warfare.

As Governor of Indiana Territory, William Henry Harrison was actively negotiating to acquire more land for settlement. He was in such sharp conflict with Tecumseh that the two nearly came to blows at one meeting. In 1811, Harrison marched on the brothers' village at a time when he knew Tecumseh was absent and defeated The Prophet at Tippecanoe. This battle did not end a war, but served as a prelude. The United States and England were already headed for war that would exploit Indian tensions.

The U.S. prepared for conflict by upgrading their forces in the Northwest. In the spring of 1812, command of the new army was offered to Michigan Territorial Governor William Hull. At that time, the only settled part of Michigan was a strip along Lake Erie from present-day Toledo to Detroit that was surrounded by the British in Canada and hostile Indians in the interior. Hull was a graduate of Yale and a Revolutionary veteran who had served with distinction, but he was now 59 and considerably more cautious. He first refused the commander's job but was persuaded to accept it when he found he did not have to relinquish his job as territorial governor. This frontier mix of civilian and military authority had failed previously. Arthur St. Clair's defeat in 1791 was one example. Also, James Wilkinson had been commander of the Army in 1806, while serving as Governor of Louisiana Territory and also working as a spy for Spain. But the choice of Hull may have been an even more disastrous decision than these two.

In June of 1812, Hull collected 2,000 troops at Urbana. His force consisted of one regiment of regular professional soldiers and three regiments of activated Ohio militia. The Ohio soldiers were untrained and undisciplined, yet their elected officers outranked the Colonel of the regular U.S. infantry regiment.

Hull's orders were to proceed to Detroit by the best route. He considered following Wayne's water-based supply route but ultimately decided to build a direct overland road. The path he built became U.S. Route 68, but he first had to make a supply route through the Black Swamp. This morass was approximately 100 miles long and 40 miles wide, and Hull detached one of the Ohio regiments to begin construction ahead of the army.

North of Bellefontaine was still considered Indian Territory that the Americans needed permission to cross. At this point near present-day Lakeview, troops under Captain James Manary had already constructed a blockhouse that became the first supply post on Hull's

The Forts of Ohio

Trace. From there, the Ohioans proceeded north 44 miles until they arrived at the upper reaches of the Scioto River.

On the south bank of the Scioto, about three miles west of the future Hardin County seat of Kenton, they stopped to build a fort. It was a small supply post that covered only about a half acre. There were blockhouses on the northwest and southeast corners only, although they were substantial twenty-foot-square buildings with second stories that projected out. The logs on the stockade wall were fifteen to eighteen inches in diameter, with the main gate on the north side facing the Scioto. Inside were barracks and storerooms with the roofs sloping inward. The fort was constructed quickly and named for regimental commander Colonel Duncan McArthur.

McArthur had served in Harmar's 1790 campaign as a teenager. He then became a surveyor and was involved in the founding of Chillicothe, where he became a wealthy land speculator and prominent politician. Later he would become a General in the army. After the War of 1812, he served as Speaker of the Ohio House, as a Congressman, and Governor of Ohio, from 1830 to 1832.

Fort McArthur was completed in time for the arrival of Hull's army on Friday, June 19. The army spent the weekend there, with a heavy rainstorm on Sunday, the 21st, guaranteeing them an extra day in camp. However, a second Ohio regiment was sent out earlier to replace McArthur's troops as road and fort builders. On June 22, the army moved out, leaving a company of 50 men under Captain Andrew Dill to garrison the new fort.

The Forts of Ohio

After Hull's disastrous defeat at Detroit, Fort McArthur was still used. In October of 1812, 1,000 militia troops under General Edward Tupper stopped at the fort on their way north. After being turned back by enemy forces on the Maumee River, Tupper's men returned in late November and spent the winter of 1812-1813 at Fort McArthur. During the harsh winter, 16 soldiers died of illness or disease and were buried nearby.

The only casualty of hostile fire at the fort was the Shawnee chief Black Hoof. A friend of the Americans, Black Hoof was meeting with Tupper when he was apparently shot and wounded by an unknown assailant.

When Tupper moved out in the spring, he left the fort under the care of Captain Robert McClelland and 127 men on May 25, 1813. This garrison remained here until November, and there was a handful of troops present until 1816, but there was no more action at Fort McArthur.

In 1913, the Daughters of the American Revolution placed a marker at the site of Fort McArthur. They also assumed care of the graves of the dead soldiers and placed several other markers along Hull's Trace.

FORT NECESSITY

On June 21, 1812, a regiment of Ohio militia under Colonel James Findlay left Fort McArthur to continue building a road to Detroit. Work went slowly in the Black Swamp region and the troops had only progressed sixteen miles before necessity dictated stopping to build a fort.

The Forts of Ohio

After fighting heavy rains, flies, and mosquitoes, the soldiers halted in what is now Madison Township in Hancock County. Here they built a small stockade with one blockhouse, and a few rude cabins. The post was to be used to store ammunition, food, and pack saddles. The small fort was christened Fort Necessity but was unofficially known as Fort Mud.

The main army under General Hull arrived here on June 24. Hull's troops moved at an even slower pace as the General, anxious to avoid the disasters that befell St. Clair, held to an specific order of march. Hull's army was not going to be surprised, but it moved very slowly.

The Americans were also hampered by incredibly poor communication. For example, they were already at war, but they didn't know it yet. Congress had declared war on June 18, but the commander of the Northwestern Army did not find this out until July 2, because the letter informing him was sent via regular mail. During this two-week lag, Hull had sent medical supplies and important papers by boat to Detroit. The British had done a better job of notification and they had naval control on the Great Lakes. They were therefore able to capture the oblivious American ships, which contained Hull's plans. This vital information was also withheld from other American officers. The commander of Fort Michilimackinac in northern Michigan found out the U.S. was at war only when told by the British officer who had surrounded his fort to successfully demand surrender.

The Forts of Ohio

When the American army left Fort Necessity, it took them three days to slog the thirteen miles to their next fort. It is not known if even a token garrison was left behind. There is no trace left of the fort today.

FORT FINDLAY

The Ohio militia regiment of Colonel James Findlay built the road for Hull's army between Forts McArthur and Findlay. A former mayor of Cincinnati, Findlay later became a Congressman and unsuccessful gubernatorial candidate. After leaving Fort Necessity, Findlay's men reached the Blanchard River on June 25. Here they built a fort that was named for their commander, as was the city that grew up on the site.

Fort Findlay was constructed on the south bank of the river, just a few blocks north of the current Hancock County courthouse. The fort was small with one account stating it was only 50 feet square, although another says it was 150 feet square. But there were four two- story blockhouses built, as well as several small cabins. The walls were of upright logs ten feet high and the main gate was on what is now the west side of Main Street. There was a ditch in front, as the fort was built a little way off the river, and the land was cleared all the way around the post.

The main army was at the uncompleted fort only briefly. While here, General Hull received a dispatch from the Secretary of War urging him to proceed to Detroit. He replied on June 26, complaining that "since the army marched from Urbana, we have had constant and heavy rains." The next day, the army pulled out, leaving completion of the fort to a garrison of just fifteen men under the command of Captain Arthur Thomas. Although boats were later built here to carry supplies to the Maumee, Fort Findlay appears to have little other military significance. No trace remains of the fort.

After leaving Fort Findlay, road-construction detail was passed on to the third regiment of Ohio militia. Led by Colonel Lewis Cass, these troops built a blockhouse where their road crossed the Portage River, about halfway between Findlay and the Maumee. Though referred to as Fort Portage, there was apparently no stockade or garrison at this supply blockhouse. This regiment also broke tradition and did not name their structure after their commanding officer, but Lewis Cass would go on to make a bigger name for himself.

A native of New England who came to Ohio as a young man, Cass would later become a general in the regular army. He also would succeed Hull as Governor of Michigan Territory. Later he would occupy such national positions as Secretary of War, Ambassador to France, and Secretary of State. And in 1848, he became the Democratic nominee for President, narrowly losing to fellow War of 1812 veteran, Zachary Taylor.

Hull's army left Fort Findlay and marched into disaster. After arriving at Detroit they crossed into Canada, but this brief invasion raised false hopes. Aggressive action by Indians under Tecumseh and British general Isaac Brock soon caused Hull to retreat to Detroit. Here the Americans were shelled by British ships in the Detroit River, throwing Hull into open panic. When the British implied they might not be able to stop an Indian massacre if there was a battle, Hull surrendered his army on August 16 without firing a shot.

Hull surrendered all of the troops under his command. Reinforcements on their way to the front were disgusted to discover their commander had surrendered them before they had a chance to fight. The loss of this army sent panic across the Ohio frontier and outrage across the country. Hull was court martialed and, although acquitted of treason, he was convicted of cowardice and dereliction of duty. He was sentenced to death but spared by order of President Madison due to his Revolutionary War service record.

FORT BARBEE

Fear gripped the Ohio frontier in the fall of 1812. Just after William Hull surrendered Detroit without a fight, the garrison of Fort Dearborn at Chicago was massacred after evacuating the fort. The only Great Lakes-area post the Americans held was Fort Wayne, and in September it was besieged.

New armies were being raised on the frontier but there was a leadership vacuum. The Madison administration followed their usual policy when they selected James Winchester as the new commander of the

Northwestern army. Winchester was another aging former Revolutionary War officer. Although he now lived in the west, Winchester was considered aristocratic and was not popular with the undisciplined militia that comprised the bulk of the army.

William Henry Harrison noted that the home-grown militia required a special hand and that they "would never do anything brilliant under a stranger." He longed for command himself and as the hero of the Battle of Tippecanoe, he was popular with the rank and file. He also had backers in Washington, such as James Monroe and Henry Clay. More immediately, he had the backing of incoming Kentucky Governor Isaac Shelby, who appointed Harrison a Major General of Kentucky militia even though Harrison was not only not a Kentucky resident but was the Governor of Indiana Territory.

This appointment enabled Harrison to spring into action immediately and hold off on accepting a federal commission that was secondary to Winchester's. Harrison moved towards Fort Wayne, where his men lifted the siege. When Winchester arrived later, Harrison turned command over to him and returned to Piqua. However, the Madison administration finally decided to make him commander in late September, although unlike Hull, he was required to resign his governorship.

Under pressure to retake Detroit before winter, Harrison organized a three-pronged assault line. The right wing was to occupy forts along the Sandusky River. This group was composed of militia from Ohio, Pennsylvania and Virginia, and would bring the first artillery into the new campaign. The center wing under General Edward Tupper's Ohio militia would occupy the forts along Hull's Trace, while the left wing would be under Winchester's command with the area around old Fort Defiance the focal spot.

The string of supply posts for this wing was to begin at the site of Wayne's Fort St. Marys, since this spot was where a water-based supply route could begin. However, the old fort was in disrepair and too small, so a new post was constructed by a Kentucky militia regiment under Colonel Joshua Barbee. These troops dismantled one of the old St. Marys blockhouses and built another one nearby.

The two forts may have overlapped slightly, but the newer, larger fort covered much of downtown St. Marys. The new fort was, like the old one, on the west bank of the St. Marys River. A second blockhouse was constructed for use as Harrison's headquarters. Work was begun in early September of 1812, but the ten-foot-high stockade wall was not added until later in the fall. Also built later on were several storage buildings and an extensive livestock corral.

The fort's water supply came from a natural spring located at the current site of the Hotel Fort Barbee, which was also called the Fountain Hotel because of the spring. The fort was named Fort Barbee in honor of the regimental commander, but was more often referred to as Fort St. Marys.

The Forts of Ohio

Over 3,000 soldiers were at the post in early October when Harrison was hoping to launch an attack on Detroit. However, bad weather and problems with supply routes made it difficult to organize any expedition. Harrison wrote to the Secretary of War, "you can scarcely form an idea, sir, of the difficulty with which land transportation is effected north of the fortieth degree of latitude in this country. The country beyond that is almost a continual swamp to the lakes."

Combined with logistical problems in the terrain were difficulties with supply contractors. A Captain Collins cut a road south from Fort Barbee to receive overland supplies from the area of old Fort Loramie. But this road was so bad that in wet weather it could take as much as two weeks for wagon convoys to travel the twelve miles. This travel was so difficult that it was said that the road could be spotted by the line of buzzards feasting on the carrion of pack horses that died along the route. Unscrupulous contractors were also suspected of driving their horses to death so they could collect inflated compensation for them from the federal government.

Harrison was not able to launch a fall offensive, but Fort Barbee became the anchor of a western supply route that followed the Auglaize River. In March of 1813, this string of outposts was placed in the hands of Ohio militia under General John Wingate, who made his headquarters at Fort Barbee. The fort was abandoned by 1814, and the site today is occupied by downtown St. Marys.

FORT AMANDA

Fort Amanda, the only military post in Ohio to be named for an eleven-year-old girl, was built by a Kentucky militia regiment under Colonel Robert Poague. In October of 1812, these troops were ordered by General Harrison to build a road between Forts Jennings and Winchester and then return south via some villages of the Ottawa tribe that were in the area. After completing this mission, they were to build a stockade on the Auglaize River, approximately twelve miles from Fort Barbee. The spot they built on is today located on State Route 198, about nine miles north of Wapakoneta in Auglaize County.

Work on the new fort went quickly and uneventfully except for the scalping of Captain Enoch Dawson, who was killed while picking grapes. The completed post was 160 feet square with four blockhouses with protruding second stories. The main gate was on the northwest wall facing the river, while another fifteen-foot-wide gate was on the southeast curtain. The stockade walls were eleven feet high with the pickets set four feet in the ground. Colonel Poague departed from Kentucky colonel tradition and declined to make his fort eponymous, and instead named the fort after his eleven-year-old daughter. Fort Amanda was then left in the hands of 64 Kentucky militia under the leadership of Captain Thompson Ward.

In February 1813, these troops were replaced by Ohio militia under Captain Daniel Hasbrook. A member of the replacement garrison wrote of the joy of the Kentuckians at being able to return home: "All in high glee and black and dirty as Indians (they) sang and danced in the most infamous manner and the most blasphemous swearing possible... to utter was made by those self-conceited infidels."

The Ohioans set about expanding the fort, doubling the size to 160 by 320 feet. They also added storage buildings, cabins, and a fifth blockhouse, as well as a corral space so large that 1,200 horses wintered there. Another addition was a hospital, which was needed in light of the diseases that were rampant among the troops. Even though there was never any combat on the site, there were 75 men who died at the fort from various causes. Contagious disease was such a problem that the fort's Fourth of July celebration in 1813 was canceled due to measles.

The Forts of Ohio

The most notable activity at Fort Amanda was boat-building. The Auglaize was a deeper river then, and boats built here could be floated to the Maumee much quicker than from Fort Barbee. The frontier boat of choice was the pirogue, a canoe made from a hollow tree trunk. Over 70 such boats were constructed here, including the ones used by the troops who reinforced Fort Meigs during the siege of May, 1813. Most boats built here, however, were used to transport supplies to the forts on up the line.

The Forts of Ohio

Although Harrison visited Fort Amanda in the summer of 1813, it was not militarily significant and was abandoned in 1814. The site stood unnoted for one hundred years until a commemorative shaft was erected in 1915.

Today Fort Amanda is a state memorial maintained by the Johnny Appleseed Metro Park District. In addition to the monument, there is a trail that goes along the river past the graves of those who died of illness here.

FORT JENNINGS

In the fall of 1812, William Henry Harrison commanded a 3,000-man force that consisted of three Kentucky militia regiments and one regiment of regular U.S. troops. While Harrison was headquartered at Fort Barbee, he ordered a militia regiment under Colonel William Jennings to build an advance post that would start to establish a supply route connection to the site of Fort Defiance. He gave this order September 21.

Jennings' men traveled 30 miles into Indian Territory currently occupied by the Ottawa tribe. Following the Auglaize River, they reached the site of the present-day Putnam County village of Fort Jennings, and began construction. They hadn't finished the job when they were joined by the rest of Harrison's army, which was hurrying north in response to rumors of a large British force on the Maumee. The entire army camped on the site on the night of October 1 in a miserable cold rain without the luxury of tents.

The Forts of Ohio

It turned out the British had left the area and there was no battle, although Harrison proceeded on to meet Winchester at Defiance. The militia returned to their duties of road and fort building. Jennings' men also built Fort Brown and Fort Junction in present day Paulding County, as way stations between Fort Jennings and Defiance. These two posts were most likely just blockhouses along the supply route.

Fort Jennings was known to have had a stockade and at least two blockhouses. The stockade enclosed about an acre and there were some cabins clustered around a spring inside and a few more cabins located outside the walls. Work was completed by mid-October and Colonel Jennings allowed the fort to be named after him. Jennings was an experienced Indian fighter, having been wounded at Harmar's and St. Clair's defeats and also having served with Harrison at Tippecanoe. He was also domineering and loud, according to one contemporary diarist, and always eager to expand his command to include visiting supply escorts.

All of the Auglaize supply forts were originally placed under the leadership of Lieutenant Colonel John Campbell of the 19th U.S. Infantry. In March of 1813, however, a change was made and all garrisons were replaced with Ohio militia under General John Wingate. The garrison duty had been dull for the Kentuckians, with few official duties other than building boats, smoking meat and making cartridges. They were relieved to be relieved and on the night of March 1, they spent their last night at Fort Jennings celebrating their imminent departure.

The Forts of Ohio

The next day, 47 men under Captain Van McHenry took over. These soldiers had to leave their baggage behind temporarily at Fort Amanda because of excessive ice on the Auglaize River. The Ohioans repaired and expanded the fort and were relieved by another fresh garrison in August. The fort was occupied until December 1814 and never saw any action, although about a dozen soldiers died here of "swamp fever".

Today, the site of Fort Jennings is noted on the west bank of the Auglaize near the junction of state routes 189 and 190 in the village of the same name. The Buckeye Trail passes this spot as it does several of the State Route 66 forts between Piqua and Defiance.

FORT WINCHESTER

The frontier forts at the "head of the line" tended to have it the worst in terms of provisions. And as the Americans' most advanced soldiers, Fort Winchester's troops suffered so much that their situation was likened to Valley Forge.

After William Henry Harrison raised the siege of Fort Wayne in September 1812, he relinquished command to General James Winchester. The troops greatly preferred Harrison over the aristocratic Winchester, but Harrison yielded gracefully and returned to Piqua. Here he learned on September 24 that the Madison Administration had decided to offer him overall command of the Northwest Army.

The Forts of Ohio

In the meantime, Winchester was cautiously advancing up the Maumee River from Fort Wayne beginning on September 22. His goal was the head of navigation at the Maumee Rapids where there was unharvested corn and where any attack on Detroit would have to begin. Winchester marched along the north bank of the river, playing a cat-and-mouse game with a large British and Indian force. The British left when they feared American reinforcements might come north from Fort Jennings and Winchester's exhausted and hungry men arrived at the site of Fort Defiance on September 30.

Harrison arrived from Fort Jennings on October 4 with 200 cattle and 200 packhorses laden with welcome supplies. Even more welcome was the news that Harrison was to be their commander, as the troops were said to be on the verge of mutiny. Winchester was so unpopular that his own men played pranks on him, such as stretching a porcupine skin across his toilet seat. After addressing the men, Harrison stayed long enough to select a location for a new fort before returning to his winter headquarters in Columbus.

Old Fort Defiance had decayed too much to be used, and it was also too small. The new fort encompassed three acres compared to the half acre of Defiance. The spot Harrison chose was a few yards below the old fort on the west bank of the Auglaize River. The site covered approximately two city blocks and ran between present-day Front and Third Streets between Washington and Jefferson Streets. The parallelogram-shaped fort was shielded from the Auglaize by a row of apple trees. To speed up the process, 250 men with axes were detailed to cut timber while the remainder of the army moved their camp closer to the site.

Work progressed quickly and the fort was completed by October 15. As a possible consolation for losing overall command, the fort was named for Winchester, although it was still frequently referred to as Fort Defiance. Fort Winchester was an impressive structure, and was even called "beautiful" by one soldier/diarist. The new fort featured four, two-story protruding blockhouses and gates on each curtain. The pointed stockade walls were twelve to fifteen feet high and there was a drainage ditch outside the walls. Inside the gates were storehouses, barracks, a hospital, and a powder magazine. A unique feature was an underground tunnel from beneath the northeast blockhouse to the river to ensure a reliable water supply.

Harrison had urged Winchester to advance to the Maumee Rapids, but rivalry between officers and supply problems made it difficult to move. Most of his men were outside the fort's gates and their plight worsened as the weather did. Their name for the fort was Fort Starvation, which was not much of an exaggeration. For over two weeks in December, the army was completely out of flour. Replacement uniforms and shoes did not arrive, so many soldiers became unfit for duty as their clothing wore out. Over 100 men died in November and December, and with three or four funerals daily, the troops' morale plummeted.

The Forts of Ohio

On December 17, a welcome herd of hogs arrived from Fort Jennings and five days later a shipment of flour arrived. On Christmas Day, the troops were finally ready to advance on the Rapids. They arrived there, unopposed, on January 10, 1813. From there, they received a request for assistance from Americans living at Frenchtown on the Raisin River in Michigan Territory. These citizens reported that a small British force was guarding a large cache of supplies not far from the American army.

At this time, Harrison was contemplating a retreat to Fort Jennings due to supply problems. But the normally slow moving Winchester now acted quickly and sent half his force on to Frenchtown where they routed the British supply convoy. Winchester and the rest of his men followed later. The Americans expected a counterattack at some point, but Winchester did not properly prepare for it and made his headquarters far in the rear at the house of a wealthy French Canadian known for his well-stocked wine cellar. When the British attacked on January 23, the unprepared Americans were thrown into confusion. When Winchester tried to make his way to the front, he was captured by Indians.

As a prisoner, Winchester could not order his troops to surrender, but he did persuade them to do so after negotiations. The Americans were holding their own in the fighting but received assurances they would be treated humanely. However, these assurances proved worthless later when Indians began to massacre American prisoners who were too wounded to travel. American casualties at the

River Raisin were around 200 killed and 750 captured, and afterwards, "Remember the River Raisin" became a rallying cry.

After this disaster, all plans for retaking Detroit had to be revised. Harrison arrived at the Maumee Rapids on February 1 and began construction of a new fort at the head of the line. Fort Winchester was still used at a supply post until 1815. There is a marker on the spot today.

FORT MEIGS

Fort Meigs was not only the largest Ohio fort of the War of 1812, but it was the host to the most action, at least in terms of noise. During a four day period in May of 1813, the British fired nearly 1,700 cannonballs at the fort in an unsuccessful siege that was a turning point in the War of 1812.

From Grand Rapids to Perrysburg, the Maumee River drops 55 feet in the space of fourteen miles. The end of these rapids marks the head of navigation for lake worthy boats. Once James Winchester occupied this important spot in January 1813, the Americans were reluctant to surrender it to the British. When Winchester went on to inglorious defeat at the River Raisin, critics of William Henry Harrison accused him of sending a potential rival to his doom. But Winchester had actually disobeyed orders by moving north without waiting for the rest of the American army.

The Forts of Ohio

Upon hearing of Winchester's defeat, Harrison retreated to the Portage River below present-day Bowling Green to await reinforcements and supplies. When no British follow-up attack materialized, Harrison advanced back to the rapids on February 1. He still hoped to advance on Detroit before the six month enlistment period of his militia ran out, but uncooperative weather made it a wiser choice to fortify his current location.

Winchester had already begun construction of a fort on the north shore of the river, but since British ships could control the river there, Harrison chose a spot on the south side where a fort could be reached by road. He selected a site on a bluff and began work on a fort that was to be named for Ohio Governor Return J. Meigs.

Previous American forts during this war had been haphazardly thrown up by militia regiments and were simple designs not capable of withstanding artillery attack. But at Fort Meigs, Harrison had available two trained military engineers who were graduates of the recently established United States Military Academy at West Point. Captain Charles Gratiot was supposed to supervise construction, but he was ill during most of this period. His duties were passed on to Captain Eleazor Wood, an 1806 West Point grad who proved to be up to the job.

However, he didn't get a lot of help from the militia that was supposed to do the construction. In March, Wood was sent to supervise improvements at nearby Fort Stephenson at about the same time that Harrison had to go to Cincinnati on personal business. When Wood returned, he was shocked to find that not only had little work been done in his absence, but the Virginia militia had actually pulled sharpened pickets out of the ground to use for firewood. Acting commander General Joel Leftwich, who Wood called a "phlegmatic, stupid old granny" did nothing to discipline his militia, reasoning that they would be leaving soon anyway as their enlistments were nearly up.

The weather was also not much help. In February, Wood described "ground so hard frozen that it was almost impossible to open it with a spade and a pickax." After the spring thaw, another diarist complained, "our camp is overwhelmed with mud and water."

Despite such setbacks, a fairly substantial fort was completed by the end of April. Like Fort Greeneville, where Harrison had served nearly twenty years previously, Fort Meigs was more of an armed camp. Built on a 40 foot high natural embankment, the fort had an irregular shape that conformed to the contours of the bluff. The circumference of the stockade was 2,500 feet, which enclosed an area of nearly ten acres. The stockade walls were fifteen feet high and planted three feet in the ground. The original design called for eight irregularly spaced blockhouses, but one of these was converted to an elevated artillery battery.

A sufficient quantity of artillery had finally been sent to the American army, so the fort had five separate batteries. There was a variety of guns, some that fired an eighteen pound cannonball, a number of six pounders, and a few howitzers. To protect the fort's gunpowder, Wood designed two underground powder magazines. Just outside the gates was a bakery, artificers' yard and slaughterhouse, and on the riverbank was a boat harbor and dock.

The soldiers lived in tents rather than barracks. The tents were arranged in orderly blocks with boulevards between them, so the fort looked like a large walled city. With a population of over 2,000, it was one of the largest cities for miles around. The soldiers/citizens of the city amused themselves by singing, drinking, and fishing. One diarist noted that when spearing fish in the Maumee he often speared two and sometimes three fish at a single stroke.

Indian war parties occasionally harassed troops who strayed too far from the fort's gates, but for the most part the bad weather hampered the enemy as much as it did the Americans. But as the fort was being completed in late April, it became apparent that Fort Meigs was to be a target. On April 24, British General Henry Procter sailed from Detroit with 1,000 British regulars and Canadian militia and heavy artillery that included 24-pounders captured in the fall of Detroit. A band of 1,200 Indian braves under Tecumseh traveled overland and met the British at the Rapids. They set up their headquarters at the site of the old abandoned Fort Miamis, across the river from Fort Meigs.

Harrison sent word to an advancing column of Kentucky militia reinforcements to hurry up and prepared for an artillery siege. The British set their artillery batteries up across the Maumee where they had a clear view of the

Americans' tents. To counter this advantage, Wood directed the garrison to dig a traverse, or wall of earth, the length of the fort. This mound was fifteen feet high and had to be constructed while Indian snipers tried to pick off the diggers. But the work was completed by the morning of May 1, when the British were about to begin their bombardment. Harrison gave the order, and in a matter of minutes, the Americans struck their tents and moved them behind the Grand Traverse, out of sight of the British.

The British began their barrage anyway, firing as many as 500 cannon balls at the fort in a day. But there were few casualties and American morale remained high. One soldier even became proficient at calling out where each cannonball was headed--until he took a direct hit himself. The Americans' cannon issued a limited response due to ammunition shortages--there were only 360 cannon balls in the fort. Harrison offered an extra ration of whiskey for every re-usable cannon ball retrieved, and by the end of the siege the Americans had actually more than when they started.

On the second day of the siege, the British began firing forge heated cannonballs in hopes of exploding the fort's powder magazines, but Wood's designs had them sufficiently protected underground. A greater threat appeared on May 3, when the British moved a battery across the river just 300 yards east of the fort. But Wood had anticipated this move and had already had new traverses built at angles that counteracted this new threat. Having a trained engineer clearly helped the Americans deal with the better equipped British invaders. The ambitious Wood rose to the rank of Colonel but was killed in battle at Fort Erie near Niagara Falls in 1814. His memory was preserved when the county where he designed his best fort was named for him.

The Indians who thirsted for blood and plunder were frustrated by slow-moving siege warfare. Tecumseh complained to the Americans that "you hide behind logs and in the earth like a groundhog" and challenged them to come out and fight. On May 4, Procter requested an American surrender saying he would not be able to restrain the Indians if the fort was taken in combat. This was the usual British threat, although it rang hollow, since at the River Raisin the Americans had agreed to surrender and had still been massacred.

Harrison derisively rejected this demand, but the Americans were still outnumbered, surrounded, and low on provisions. So it was with great relief that Harrison learned on May 4th that 1,200 Kentucky militia under General Green Clay were just a few miles upstream. Harrison devised a plan where they were to shoot the rapids the next morning and split into two groups. Clay and 400 men were to land on the south bank and fight their way to the fort, while the other 800 under Colonel William Dudley were to attack the British batteries on the other side of the river. They were given spikes to drive into the cannon, rendering them useless, and were told to return to the fort immediately afterwards. Meanwhile, a group under Colonel John Miller of the 19th regiment of regulars would sally from the fort and attack the battery on the American side of the river.

Everything worked according to plan, with one disastrous exception. While engaged in spiking enemy guns, Dudley's force was distracted by Indians firing at them and responded by chasing them into the woods. While the garrison helplessly watched them disobey orders, the Kentuckians were lured into a trap and cut off. Only about 150 of Dudley's 800 men made it back to the fort, with most of the remainder taken prisoner.

The captives were robbed of money and clothing and made to run Indian gauntlets. They were taken to old Fort Miamis where Indians fired into groups of them and then began to pick out victims to tomahawk and scalp. About 40 Americans were murdered this way until an outraged Tecumseh rode up and upbraided Procter for doing nothing to stop the murders. Procter replied, "Your Indians cannot be commanded." Tecumseh angrily retorted, "You are unfit to command. Go and put on petticoats."

The American losses from the fighting on May 5th were heavy. In addition to Dudley's losses, the Americans in the fort had 80 killed and 189 wounded. But they still held the fort and the British alliance began to crack. The Indians had their fill of fighting, and having little patience for siege warfare, began to drift off. The Canadian militia wanted to go home and plant their spring crops. And on May 7th, Procter learned that Fort York at Toronto had fallen to the Americans, which made him fear attack from another direction. Although he renewed his surrender demand that day, Procter knew he would have to abandon the siege. After a prisoner exchange, Procter sailed off on May 9, with the victorious American forces firing a final artillery salvo as the British left. Before Fort Meigs, the American Army of the Northwest had not won a single battle. After Fort Meigs, they never lost one.

After the siege, Harrison moved to other sectors, leaving the fort under Clay's command. On July 20, the garrison again spied British sails on the river. This time the invading force was comprised of only 350 regular British troops but over 3,000 Indians. But most British artillery was unavailable as it was needed to outfit the fleet preparing to do battle with Commodore Perry. And small arms fire by Indian snipers was ineffective against veterans who were now battle hardened. One member of the garrison observed, "Never did I expect to see men grow so indifferent to the sound of bullets. ...Here, if a man has his glass of grog shattered as he passes it to his lips, it is treated with derision."

The Americans were expecting an assault at any moment, but instead, on the afternoon of July 25, they heard the distant sounds of battle coming from the road to the Sandusky forts. The troops were convinced that their reinforcements were under attack and wanted to rush to their aid. But General Clay was not expecting reinforcements for a few days, and, suspecting a trap, refused to be drawn out of the fort. In fact, it was a sham battle set up by Tecumseh's braves to try to lure the ground hogs out from behind their logs. When the

The Forts of Ohio

Americans refused to fall for the trap, the British sailed off to attack the smaller Fort Stephenson on July 28.

In mid-August, a less threatened Fort Meigs was reduced in size to a 150 foot square stockade. The existing northwest blockhouse was kept and a new 14 foot high wall built around it and three new blockhouses. The new version was surrounded by a ditch six feet deep and five feet wide with earth mounded up towards the pickets. Barracks and storehouses were added and on September 5th the fort was left under the command of General Duncan McArthur. After Perry's victory on Lake Erie, all but about 80 soldiers were sent to Canada with the rest of Harrison's army. After Harrison defeated Procter there, Fort Meigs was kept as a supply base and manned by a small contingent of Ohio militia. The fort was finally abandoned in May 1815.

Fort Meigs did play host to one more major event, and it involved over 25,000 people. The occasion was a political rally for Presidential candidate Harrison in 1840 at the site of his victory. Despite being the son of a wealthy plantation owner who signed the Declaration of Independence, Harrison's opponents tried to portray him as a rube who only wanted to drink hard cider in his log cabin. Harrison's supporters made these negatives into positives and used hard cider and log cabins as symbols of their man's grass roots appeal.

The Fort Meigs rally was one of the largest of an aggressive campaign that landed Harrison in the White House. The rally was a reunion of 1812 veterans and featured music, parades, artillery salutes and lots of cider.

The Forts of Ohio

Harrison died in office after serving only six weeks as President, but he was one of several 1812 veterans to be on a national ticket. Andrew Jackson and Zachary Taylor were two officers who became president, although Taylor was more known for his service in the War with Mexico. Richard Mentor Johnson, who commanded a mounted regiment under Harrison at the Battle of the Thames, was elected Vice President in 1836, with his biggest claim to fame being that he allegedly killed Tecumseh in that battle. Winfield Scott, also known primarily for his Mexican experience, was the Democratic nominee for president in 1852. And in 1848, the Democratic nominee was Lewis Cass, formerly of the Ohio militia, who narrowly lost to Taylor.

Today, a rebuilt Fort Meigs is a gateway site of the Ohio Historical Society. The replica features demonstrators and hosts reenactment activities. Located just off State Route 25 below Perrysburg, the site also features a museum that opened in 2003.

FORT FEREE

The right wing of Harrison's northwestern army was late getting into the action, but once these Sandusky River forts got involved they played a key role in ridding Ohio of British and Indian invaders. The first link in the chain of forts along the Sandusky was Fort Feree in what is now the town of Upper Sandusky. It was here that Harrison wrote to the Secretary of War on October 15, 1812, "I have directed blockhouses to be built here for a principle deposit."

As the call went out for militia in the fall of 1812, soldiers came from other states as well as Ohio and Kentucky. A major contingent of state militia came from Virginia. These troops traveled through Ohio by way of Chillicothe, Columbus, Worthington, and Delaware before arriving at Upper Sandusky. Another group of Pennsylvania militia arrived at the same spot by way of Pittsburgh, Canton, Wooster, and Mansfield. These men brought the first American artillery to the campaign, adding a much needed dimension to the war effort.

There was also a large number of Ohio militia that gathered at the mustering-in point. In fact, at one time the location was referred to as Grand Camp Ohio Militia. As the camp farthest from the front, it was at first an unorganized jumble of men and supplies and at times it seemed the men were intent only on quarreling amongst themselves and consuming the provisions that were needed closer to the front.

By January of 1813 things were better organized and at that time the Virginia militia under General Joel Leftwich were ordered to the Maumee Rapids. Approximately 700 Pennsylvania militia under General Richard Crooks remained behind to complete the fort, and with the building of a stockade, the camp became Fort Feree. The walls were of both split and round timbers and enclosed a large spring. Blockhouses were erected at each corner as well as extensive barracks and a hospital. The fort was between present-day Walker Street and Wyandot Avenue in Upper Sandusky. The cemetery for soldiers who died of illness was near the current Wyandot County Court House.

Crooks' men worked quickly to complete the fort and were sent on to Fort Meigs, where they arrived on February 20. Fort Feree continued to serve as a preliminary gathering spot and hosted large concentrations of troops at various times. On May 13, just as the first siege of Fort Meigs was ending, there were over one thousand men present at Fort Feree awaiting orders. The troops here were not all state militia, as the next month 300 regulars under Colonel Anderson of the 24th U.S. regiment were stationed here. General Harrison also used Fort Feree as a headquarters at various times during the 1813 campaign. A supply road was built north of the fort along the river to deliver supplies to posts further up the line.

Though many soldiers passed through here, Fort Feree was too far from the front to be threatened. It was abandoned as unneeded after the war.

FORT BALL

While most Ohio forts in the War of 1812 were named for militia infantry officers, Fort Ball honored a cavalry officer from the regular army. Colonel James Ball was the leader of Harrison's cavalry and the officer in charge of building the supply road that connected the various outposts along the Sandusky River. He was also the supervisor of the construction project that changed this site from a camp to a fort.

The area now occupied by the city of Tiffin was first used as a camp by militia from Ohio's Western Reserve early in 1813. From this point it was only forty miles overland from Fort Meigs, so it could serve as a good fallback location should the posts farther downstream to the north be captured. In July 1813, Ball was ordered to fortify this supply outpost.

Ball had his stockade built around a large spring on the west side of the river. The three blockhouses all faced the river, with one each at the northeast and southeast corners and one in the middle. The pickets for the stockade were twelve inches around and soil was piled up around them, which left a ditch around the fort's perimeter. The area enclosed was large enough for 500 men.

Fort Ball was never threatened by attack, but immediately after he completed construction, Ball was ordered to Fort Stephenson, where an attack was imminent. In fact, Ball carried orders for the commander to evacuate that fort in the face of overwhelming numbers. En route to this task, Ball's calvary was attacked by Indians and in the fight they managed to kill 17 Indians without losing a man.

After the British and Indians failed to take Fort Stephenson in August, additional Kentucky militia arrived at Fort Ball. A large force under the command of Kentucky Governor Isaac Shelby was here when word was received of Oliver Hazard Perry's victory on Lake Erie. Shelby was one of many Revolutionary War veterans who served in the War of 1812, but he was one of the few who served with distinction in both conflicts.

At the beginning of the war, Americans naturally offered commission to former officers from the Revolution. But these men had not served in over thirty years and in many cases were not up to the rigors of frontier fighting. Men like Hull, Winchester, and Henry Dearborn, who had all been junior officers previously, fared poorly as commanders. Even James Wilkinson was given another opportunity for independent command. But his invasion of Canada was marred by quarrels with officers, disobedience of orders, rumors of drunkenness, and a mysterious illness that appeared right before an unsuccessful battle and disappeared right afterwards.

Shelby was a rare exception to this trend. But then he was an experienced frontier fighter, having first served at the battle of Point Pleasant in 1774. During the Revolution, he was one of the leaders of the "over mountain men" that defeated a British-led Tory force at King's Mountain in 1780. He was elected the first governor of the new state of Kentucky in 1792, but then retired from politics until the War of 1812 began. He was then re-elected to the governorship, and was a strong supporter of his fellow frontier governor Harrison. When more state militia were called out, he insisted on leading them personally. At age 62, he was still robust and aggressive, and served with distinction at the Battle of the Thames before retiring for good.

After the war, a town known as Fort Ball grew around the ruins of the fort. This community was a rival of neighboring Tiffin for a Seneca County seat, but today the towns are merged under the name of Tiffin. Some of the soldiers who had served at Fort Ball later returned to settle here. In 1833, many of them attended a twenty-year reunion at the fort site. At that time it was noted that a sycamore tree was growing out of what had once been the stockade wall. That tree is still standing today, with a marker and surrounded by a fence. Also at the site is a historical marker and the statue of an Indian maiden who presides over the fort's spring.

FORT SENECA

You won't find the site of Fort Seneca in the town of Fort Seneca. It is in the nearby town of Old Fort that you will find the site of the old fort, on the west bank of the Sandusky River. And, like other Sandusky River forts, it spent more time as a camp than it did as a fort.

Originally started as a supply depot and training ground by Ohio militia, the site was not enclosed by a stockade until July 1813. At that time, a large area encompassing about one and a half acres was enclosed on a bank about forty feet above the river. The square fort featured oak pickets one foot thick and twelve feet high. There was a double row of pickets on the east side facing the river, a ravine on the south side and ditches on the north and west sides. The largest blockhouse was on the southwest corner and was twenty feet square and 16 feet high. There were smaller blockhouses on the southeast and northwest corners, while the northeast bastion contained the fort's powder magazine. The fort's water supply came from a good spring located within the walls. The name came from the Indian tribe that inhabited the area.

Fort Seneca served as General Harrison's headquarters from July to September, 1813, when the scene of action had shifted to the Americans' right wing. From Fort Seneca, there was an overland route to Fort Meigs, which could be used if Fort Stephenson, the northernmost Sandusky River post, were captured. In fact, Harrison felt that smaller Fort Stephenson was indefensible, and therefore expendable. He ordered it abandoned in the face of British invasion, but word was received too late for evacuation.

At that time, the garrison at Fort Seneca contained 800 men, consisting of one fifth cavalry and the rest militia. This was not a large enough force to confront the combined British and Indian attackers who surrounded the 160-man garrison at Fort Stephenson. So on August 1, they stayed put and could hear the cannon fire from the assault on Fort Stephenson. The tiny American garrison repulsed the attackers on their own, however, and the British had to sail away in defeat.

Afterwards, the campaign in the northwest switched to the naval theater. Commodore Perry had finally completed construction of a fleet at Erie, Pennsylvania, and was ready to challenge the British fleet for control of Lake Erie. After Perry launched his fleet, he sent an invitation to Harrison at Fort Seneca to come for an inspection. On August 20, he met Perry for a tour, accompanied by the 72 year old chief Tarhe (The Crane) of the Wyandot tribe.

Tarhe had fought against Harmar, St. Clair and Wayne, but after signing the Greeneville Treaty, had become an ally of the Americans. At a conference with Harrison in Columbus in June 1813, Tarhe had complained that while the British actively sought Indians to fight for them, the Americans were refusing to let pro-American Indians fight for them. Harrison brought the chief with him in an effort to include Indian allies in the American effort

The Forts of Ohio

At this time, the garrison at Fort Seneca also provided manpower for Perry, who was desperately in need of sailors. A contingent of about 100 men volunteered for naval duty and after a brief tour and orientation, became a major part of Perry's crew. The landlubbers handled the ship's guns well when Perry met the British fleet near Put-In-Bay on September 10, 1813. After several hours of fierce fighting, one of the most famous messages in American history was delivered to Harrison at Fort Seneca. Perry reported, "We have met the enemy and they are ours" and his success led to an invasion of Canada and ultimate American victory.

Today, a small replica of a log blockhouse is in the village park of Old Fort a mile or so east of State Route 53.

FORT STEPHENSON

The last fort in Ohio to be attacked was just a few miles from the first one. But the result was completely different than when Fort Sandusky was captured in 1763, exactly 50 years earlier. This time the garrison completely routed the attackers in as decisive a victory that ever occurred in Ohio.

The location of Fort Stephenson in present-day Fremont had been a significant one going back to the early days of Ohio forts. Vessels traveling on Lake Erie could go up the Sandusky River this far before having to unload their cargo. As the head of navigation, the spot became an important transfer point on the route between Pittsburgh and Detroit. Known as Lower Sandusky because it was downstream from Upper Sandusky, it became an important trading point. During the American Revolution, captives of the Indians were brought here where the more fortunate were sent on to Detroit for adoption or exchange. The less fortunate were burned at the stake here.

During the War of 1812, the site became important again, when the most forward of the Sandusky River forts was naturally built here. Like most forts along this river, the status as a fort evolved gradually. In the summer of 1812, Major Thomas Butler, a veteran of Anthony Wayne's campaign, selected the site. Troops under the command of a Captain Norton of Connecticut began building an outpost around an old Indian trading post. They had blockhouses and most of the picketing done within twenty-five days, but the project and the site were abandoned in the panic after Hull's surrender of Detroit in August.

The area was not reoccupied until December when Ohio militia under the command of General Simon Perkins arrived. The next month militia under Colonel Mills Stephenson completed the fort and named it after their commander. At this time, the fort covered about an acre of ground with a stockade wall over ten feet high and eighteen inches thick. There was one blockhouse on the northeast corner and another in the center of the north wall. The fort, which was on the west bank of the river, also contained military storehouses, and a powder magazine. The main gate was at the southwest corner. In February of 1813, General Harrison sent Captain Eleazor Wood to Fort Stephenson, and this West Point-trained engineer further strengthened the fort's defenses.

After the British failure in the first siege of Fort Meigs, Harrison became convinced that the smaller outpost at Fort Stephenson would be a likely future target, since it could also be approached from Lake Erie. In July, he assigned one of his favorite officers to the post: Major George Croghan. Though only 21 years old, Croghan was a natural leader with impressive family credentials. Among his uncles were Revolutionary War hero George Rogers Clark and William Clark, the former western explorer and current Governor of Missouri Territory.

Croghan had graduated from William and Mary College and returned to his native Kentucky to practice law. But like Harrison, who had originally intended to study medicine, he found the lure of military life too strong to resist. In 1811, he enlisted as a private and fought with Harrison in the Tippecanoe campaign. He impressed Harrison and was made an aide-to-camp and then stayed in the regular army as an officer. He avoided capture at the River Raisin fiasco because he was left behind in command of Fort Winchester, and at Fort Meigs he distinguished himself in a successful assault on a British artillery battery, which earned him a promotion.

Work had continued on strengthening Fort Stephenson before Croghan's arrival. But all efforts were halted on July 4th so that the garrison could properly celebrate the holiday. The main oration was delivered by Colonel Richard Mentor Johnson, leader of a Kentucky cavalry regiment. As a former Congressman and future Vice President, Johnson was an accomplished speaker who delivered a rousing speech. The ceremonies were capped by a firing of the fort's only cannon, a six pounder affectionately known as Old Betsy.

Croghan arrived on July 15 and continued to add on to, and strengthen, the fort. He originally wanted to move the fort to a nearby hill that was better situated then the low-lying area currently occupied. But there was no time for that, so Croghan focused on adding a blockhouse on the southwest corner and digging a ditch eight feet deep and eight feet wide around the fort's perimeter.

This work was completed just in time, as on July 28, the British and Indians abandoned a second siege of Fort Meigs and headed for Fort Stephenson. The British, with

350 redcoats, sailed by way of Lake Erie and Sandusky Bay, while nearly 3,000 Indians under Tecumseh traveled overland. Harrison realized that the vulnerable fort was not militarily significant enough to justify defending and he ordered Croghan to abandon and burn it and then rejoin him at Fort Seneca.

But his messengers got lost and did not arrive at Fort Stephenson until the morning of July 30th. Croghan remembered that the garrison at Fort Dearborn in Chicago had been wiped out in open ground after evacuating the fort. With a large party of Indians rumored to be nearby he did not want to repeat that mistake. He replied to Harrison that the orders were "received too late to be carried into execution" and added "we have determined to maintain this place, and by heavens we can."

Though his reasoning was sound, Croghan's tone was insolent, and he was summoned to Harrison's headquarters at Fort Seneca to explain himself. Croghan explained that he expected his message to be captured and that he therefore had written it with a British audience in mind. He was permitted to return to command at Fort Stephenson, since small parties could still safely go between forts without attracting attention. But his orders still stood to evacuate as soon as possible.

However, on July 31, British warships were sighted and Indians outside the fort began to show themselves openly. The next day, the British began to set up artillery on shore and requested a parley to discuss surrender. Croghan sent out Lieutenant Edmund Shipp under a flag of truce to meet with British officers who urged the Americans to surrender to avoid being massacred. Shipp replied that the only way they could take the fort would be if that there was no one left to massacre. As he was attempting to return to the fort, an Indian tried to grab Shipp's sword. As the two grappled, Croghan, who was watching from the fort, shouted, "Shipp, come in and we will blow them all to hell."

Immediately afterwards, the British began their bombardment with gunboats stationed in the river and a battery of six-pounders and howitzers on land. They continued their barrage into the night, though with little effect. In returning fire, Croghan moved Old Betsy around to different locations in the fort to make the British think he had more than just one cannon.

With only 160 men under his command, Croghan was outnumbered by approximately twenty to one. But the rules that applied throughout the story of all Ohio forts were still in effect: the odds meant little if the fort was well-built and supplied. The Indians had the advantage in woodland combat, especially with their current numbers, but Croghan was not coming out to fight them. But with the noise of the bombardment, the Indians hoped to attract reinforcements that they could attack. Tecumseh and 2,000 warriors had positioned themselves along the military road so that they could accost relief parties from either Fort Seneca or Fort Meigs. Harrison had 800 men at Fort Seneca, not enough to risk open combat, so no relief was sent.

The Forts of Ohio

The other major factor in fort combat was artillery, which the British had in abundance. But their 24-pounders and other big guns were currently being loaded onto the ships that were soon to fight Perry's fleet. Captain Wood reassured Harrison that the recently reinforced fort could hold out against the lighter British guns. So even though they could hear the cannonade from Fort Seneca, Croghan was left on his own.

During the night, the British had moved a battery to within 250 yards of the fort. But their fire still failed to breach the fort's walls and by the afternoon of August 2, the British decided to resort to a direct assault. Croghan had noticed that the British had concentrated their fire on the northwest corner, and he correctly assumed that the assault would be made there. He had Old Betsy taken to the north blockhouse that overlooked the ditch and loaded the cannon with grape shot and whatever scrap metal he could find.

Around 5 p.m., a British column approached the fort through smoke so thick they were not be seen until they were within 20 feet from the fort. As the British entered the ditch, the porthole was removed from the north blockhouse and Old Betsy poured a devastating fire into the ditch from just thirty feet away. The British were forced to retreat, leaving their dead and dying scattered throughout the ditch. In the attack on the fort, the British had suffered over 100 casualties, while the American losses were one man killed and seven wounded.

That night, the British sailed away in defeat and the Americans had a new hero at a time when the war was going badly for them. Because of his youth and defiance and casualty-free victory against overwhelming numbers, Croghan became a hero overnight. Harrison was criticized for originally ordering the fort evacuation but all of his officers, including Croghan, came to his defense.

After Perry's victory on Lake Erie the next month, the American groundhogs were free to come out of their forts and invade Canada. At the Battle of the Thames on October 5, they met the British and Indians on open ground and defeated them, killing Tecumseh in the process. Never again would Ohio be invaded by European powers or attacked by Indians and never again would log forts be needed here for protection.

Croghan was promoted and given greater responsibilities as a result of his victory. He remained in the army until 1817 and after trying civilian life, he re-enlisted in 1824. He became Inspector General of the United States Army and fought in the War with Mexico, but he was similar to his uncle, George Rogers Clark, in that his greatest military moments came while he was in his 20s. He was also like his uncle in that in his later years his biggest battle was with the bottle. There is an unconfirmed story that he was to be court martialed for drunkenness but the proceedings were stopped by President Andrew Jackson. A fellow War of 1812 veteran, Jackson is alleged to have thundered, "George Croghan shall get drunk every day of his life if he wants to, and by the Eternal, the United States shall pay for the whiskey."

Croghan died in New Orleans in 1849, but he remains memorialized at the site of his greatest victory. The site of Fort Stephenson today is occupied by the Birchard Public Library in downtown Fremont. In addition to a Croghan marker, Old Betsy is also on display on the library lawn, so the two biggest heroes of the last fort to be attacked in Ohio are memorialized together.

OTHER FORTS

There were other militia-built forts in Ohio that did not figure in military campaigns. One example was Fort Huntington, built at what is now West 6th Street and Lakeside Avenue in downtown Cleveland. This fort was erected in the aftermath of the American surrender of

Detroit by soldiers under Captain Stanton Sholes. The fort was strengthened in the summer of 1813 and held by 200 men under Major Thomas Jessup.

Secretary of War John Armstrong wanted Harrison to make Cleveland his headquarters, since the mouth of the Cuyahoga was equidistant to Fort Meigs and Erie, Pennsylvania, where Perry was building his fleet. Harrison resisted this idea, as he felt the British were more likely to attack his men and forts in the Sandusky and Maumee regions. He did visit here in June of 1813, but Fort Seneca was his main headquarters.

There was no military action at Fort Huntington, although British warships were sighted offshore on June 13, 1813. The only time the fort's artillery was used, it turned out to be an American boat that was fired on. But Cleveland could well have been a military target due to its location. In no other war were so many major North American cities the scenes of battle. Buffalo, Toronto, and Washington were all captured and burned during the War of 1812, and in Chicago the fort's garrison was massacred. Detroit was captured without a fight, but Baltimore and New Orleans held out with heroic efforts from the defenders.

Today the site of Fort Huntington is marked by a stone in Huntington Park next to the Cuyahoga County Courthouse.

Another little-used fort was Fort Morrow near Waldo in Morrow County. This post was built by militia under a Captain Taylor in 1812. The stockade was built around Wyatt's Tavern, a brick building that was a local landmark. The stockade was eight feet high and made of split slats of sharpened oak. There were blockhouses at the northeast and southwest corners. There was no action here, although 13 soldiers died of various illnesses while serving here.

Fort Morrow was far from the front, although along the route that soldiers would use to get to the action. It was located along the Greeneville Treaty line, which meant it was on the border between settled Ohio and Indian country, so the location was of psychological significance.

In 1974 an archaeological expedition located the site of Wyatt's Tavern and found artifacts from the fort years. Today a marker along Route 23 in southern Morrow County shows the location of the fort.

The Forts of Ohio

On the western end of the Greenville Treaty line in Darke County there were several outposts that were referred to as forts. At New Madison, Fort Black was built by Lieutenant James Black of the Preble County militia in the fall of 1813. It is not certain whether this defensive post was enclosed by a stockade or was a blockhouse only. This is also true of Fort Nesbit in southwest Darke County, which was built by James Nesbit of the Ohio militia. There is a historical marker on the site, but even less is known about Fort Brier, another Darke County site.

Closer to the action was Fort Avery on the east bank of the Huron River in Erie County, but this was known to be a blockhouse only. Other forts built by Anthony Wayne were put back into use even though they may have deteriorated, as they could still serve to store supplies. The sites of Forts Piqua, Loramie, and Greeneville were all revived for this purpose.

There were several other blockhouses and military locations that served limited roles throughout the state, but these were the main ones with any claims to being forts.

Fort name	County	When built	Built by	Designer	Commander	Garrison	Abandoned
Sandoski	Erie	??, 1751	?	?	?	20	1754
Sandusky	Ottawa	Aug., 1761	Bouquet	Meyer	Pauli	15	1763
Gower	Athens	Sept., 1774	Dunmore	Crawford	Dunmore	100	1774
Laurens	Tuscarawas	Nov., 1778	McIntosh	Cambray-Digny	J. Gibson	180	1779
Harmar	Washington	Oct., 1785	Harmar	Doughty	Doughty	200	1795
Finney	Hamilton	Oct., 1785	Harmar	Finney	Finney	70	1787
Steuben	Jefferson	Oct., 1786	Harmar	Hamtramck	Hamtramck	200	1787
Washington	Hamilton	Aug., 1789	Harmar	Ferguson	St. Clair	500	1804
Hamilton	Butler	Oct., 1791	St. Clair	Ferguson	Armstrong	100	1796
Jefferson	Darke	Oct., 1791	St. Clair	Ferguson	Shaylor	100	1795
St. Clair	Preble	Mar., 1792	Wilkinson	Thorp	Gano	200	1795
GreenVille	Darke	Nov., 1793	Wayne	Burbeck	Wayne	3500	1796
Recovery	Mercer	Dec., 1793	Wayne	Burbeck	A. Gibson	200	1796
Adams	Mercer	Aug., 1794	Wayne	Burbeck	Underhill	40	1795
Defiance	Defiance	Aug., 1794	Wayne	Burbeck	Hunt	200	1796
Deposit	Lucas	Aug., 1794	Wayne	Burbeck	Pike	200	1794

Fort name	County	When built	Built by	Designer	Commander	Garrison	Abandoned
Miamis	Lucas	Aug., 1794	Simcoe	Pilkington	Campbell	250	1796
Piqua	Miami	Oct., 1795	Wayne	Burbeck	Salmon	?	1796
Loramie	Shelby	Oct., 1795	Wayne	Burbeck	Butler	?	1796
St. Marys	Auglaize	Oct., 1795	Wayne	Burbeck	Whistler	?	1796
Industry	Lucas	June, 1805	?	?	?	?	1805
McArthur	Hardin	June, 1812	Hull	McArthur	Dill	127	1816
Necessity	Hancock	June, 1812	Hull	Findlay	?	?	1815
Findlay	Hancock	June, 1812	Hull	Findlay	Thomas	15	1815
Barbee	Auglaize	Sept., 1812	Harrison	Barbee	Wingate	3000	1814
Amanda	Auglaize	Oct., 1812	Harrison	Poague	Ward	64	1814
Jennings	Putnam	Sept., 1812	Harrison	Jennings	McHenry	47	1814
Winchester	Defiance	Oct., 1812	Harrison	Harrison	Winchester	1000	1815
Meigs	Wood	Feb., 1813	Harrison	Wood	Harrison	2000	1815
Feree	Wyandot	Oct., 1812	Harrison	Crooks	Anderson	300	1815
Ball	Seneca	July, 1813	Harrison	Ball	Ball	500	1815
Seneca	Seneca	July, 1813	Harrison	Harrison	Harrison	800	1815
Stephenson	Sandusky	Jan., 1813	Harrison	Wood	Croghan	160	1815

GLOSSARY

Terms used in forts and military affairs of the era that are employed in this book:

artificer-- a skilled laborer such as a blacksmith or butcher who served with the army. Soldiers were used for these positions when possible, but it was often neccesary to hire civilian contractors to fill these needs.

bastion-- the projecting part at the corner of a fortification. Blockhouses were usually built here, but bastions could also be used for other purposes, like artillery platforms.

battery-- an emplacement for one or more cannon.

blockhouse-- a defensive building with loopholes for firing out of, often with a projecting second story. Could be built at corners or along walls of forts or to stand alone without a stockade wall.

curtain-- the part of a stockade wall between bastions.

fort-- defined here as a permanent stockaded army post with troops.

militia-- a military force consisting of citizens called out in times of emergency. As temporary soldiers, militia were considered less reliable and more undisciplined than regular troops.

palisade or stockade wall-- a fence of sharpened log pickets that form the outer wall of a fort.

powder magazine-- a building for storing a fort's gunpowder and ammunition supply. Powder magazines had to be kept dry and away from fire.

regulars-- professional soldiers who were members of a permanent standing army.

sally port-- a gate in a fort designed for sending out sorties.

SELECTED BIBLIOGRAPHY

Blue, Herbert T.O. *Centennial History of Hardin County, Ohio.* Canton: Rogers Miller Co., 1933.

Boatner, Mark M. *Encyclopedia of the American Revolution.* New York: David McKay Co., 1974.

Buchman, Randall L. *The Confluence: The Site of Fort Defiance.* Defiance, Ohio: Defiance College Press, 1994.

Cleaves, Freeman. *Old Tippecanoe: William Henry Harrison and His Time.* Port Washington, New York: Kennikat Press, 1939.

De Regnaucourt, Tony. *The Archaeology of Fort Recovery, Ohio.* Arcanum, Ohio: Upper Miami Valley Archaeological Research Museum, 1996.

De Regnaucourt, Tony and Paulette Hoelscher. *The Archaeology of Fort St. Marys* Arcanum, Ohio: Upper Miami Valley Archaeological Research Museum, 1996.

Elwer, Imogene. *Historical Fort Jennings. Fort Jennings, Ohio:* Fort Jennings Bicentennial Commission, 1976.

Frohman, Charles E. *Sandusky's Yesterdays.* Columbus: The Ohio Historical Society, 1968.

The Forts of Ohio

Gilpin, Alec R. *The War of 1812 in the Old Northwest.* Ann Arbor: Michigan State University Press, 1958.

Goodnough, David. *Pontiac's War.* New York: Franklin Watts, 1970.

Gottfried, Ray. *Pictorial Memories: Upper Sandusky, Wyandot County.* Upper Sandusky, 1976.

Gramly, Richard Michael. *Fort Laurens 1778-1779: The Archaeological Record* Richmond: William Byrd Pr., 1978.

Guthman, William H. *March to Massacre: A History of the First Seven Years of the United States Army* New York: McGraw Hill, 1975.

Heitman, Francis B. *Historical Register Dictionary of the United States Army.* Genealogical Publishing Co, 1903.

Hill, Leonard U. *John Johnston and the Indians in the Land of the Three Miamis.* Piqua, Ohio: Stoneman Press, 1957.

Hochsteter, Nancy. *Travel Historic Ohio: A Guide to Historical Sites and Markers. Madison,* Wisconsin: Guide Press Co., 1986.

Holmes, John R. *The Story of Fort Steuben.* Steubenville, Ohio: Fort Steuben Press, 2000.

The Forts of Ohio

Jacobs, James R. *The Beginning of the United States Army 1783-1812*. Princeton, New Jersey: Princeton University Press, 1947.

Jones, Robert Ralston. *Fort Washington at Cincinnati, Ohio*. Cincinnati: Society of Colonial Wars in the State of Ohio, 1902.

Knopf, Richard C. *Anthony Wayne and the Founding of the United States Army.* Columbus: Anthony Wayne Parkway Board, 1961.

Knopf, Richard C., ed. *Document Transcriptions of the War of 1812 in the Northwest* (12 vols). Columbus: Ohio Historical Society, 1957.

Lang, William *History of Seneca County.* Springfield, Ohio: Transcript Printing, 1980.

Lossing, Benson. *The Pictorial Fieldbook of the War of 1812*. New York: Harper and Bros., 1868.

McAfee, Robert Breckinridge. *History of the Late War in the Western Country.* Lexington, Kentucky: Worsley and Smith, 1816.

Nelson, Larry L. *Men of Patriotism, Courage, and Enterprise: Fort Meigs in the War of 1812* Bowie, Maryland: Heritage Books, 1985.

The Forts of Ohio

Ohio Historical Society. Ohio Archaeological and Historical Quarterly. Columbus, Ohio Historical Society, 1887-1934.

Pieper, Thomas I. and James B. Gidney. *Fort Laurens 1778-1779- The Revolutionary War in Ohio.* Kent: Kent State University Press, 1976.

Prucha, Francis Paul. *The Sword of the Republic: The United States Army on the Frontier 1783-1846.* London: Macmillan Co., 1969.

Rajtar, Steve. *Indian War Sites: A Guidebook to Battlefields, Monuments, and Memorials.* Jefferson, North Carolina: McFarland and Co., 1999.

Scamyhorn, Richard and John Steinle. *Stockades in the Wilderness: The Frontier Defenses and Settlements of Southwestern Ohio 1788-95.* Dayton: Landfall Press, 1986.

Simmons, David A. *The Forts of Anthony Wayne* Fort Wayne: Historical Fort Wayne, Inc., 1977.

Slocum, Charles Elihu. *The Ohio Country Between the Years 1783 and 1815.* New York: Putnam and Sons, 1910.

Smith, Thomas H., ed. *Ohio in the American Revolution* Columbus: Ohio Historical Society, 1976.

The Forts of Ohio

Stotz, Charles M. *Outposts of the War for Empire.*
Pittsburgh: Historical Soc. of Western Pennsylvania, 1985.

Sword, Wiley. *President Washington's Indian War: The Struggle for the Old Northwest 1790-1795.* Norman, Oklahoma: University of Oklahoma Press, 1985.

Tanner, Helen Hornbeck. *Atlas of Great Lakes Indian History.* Norman, Oklahoma: University of Oklahoma Press, 1987.

Van Every, Dale. *Ark of Empire, the American Frontier, 1784-1803.* New York: Morrow, 1963.

Wilson, Frazier E. *Advancing the Ohio Frontier.* Columbus: Long's College Book Co., 1953.

Wilson, Frazier E. *Around the Council Fire* Mt. Vernon, Indiana: Windmill Publications, 1975.

Wilson, Frazier E. *Fort Jefferson: The Frontier Post of the Upper Miami Valley.* Evansville, Indiana: Darke Co. Historical Society, repr. 1984.

Wood, Eleazar D. *Journal of the Northwestern Campaign of 1812-1813.* Defiance, Ohio: Defiance College Press, 1975.

Zimmer, Louise. *True Tales of Pioneer Times.* Marietta: Broughton Foods, Co., 1987.

INDEX

The Forts of Ohio

Wicked Winds:

Ohio and the 1965 Palm Sunday Tornadoes

By Roger Pickenpaugh

On April 11, 1965, an outbreak of 37 tornadoes struck six states, leaving 258 people dead, injuring thousands, and causing tens of millions of dollars in property damage.

The Night of the Wicked Winds tells the story of the six deadly tornadoes that struck Ohio that night. Based on over 125 interviews and numerous newspaper accounts, it describes the death and destruction that the storms produced, along with remarkable tales of survival. It also tells how neighbors came together to rescue the injured and rebuild devastated communities.

To order, please send $18 per copy to:

Pickenpaugh Books
501 Oaklawn Avenue
Caldwell, OH 43724

Ohio residents please add 6 1/2% sales tax. There is no charge for postage.